Love and
the Quest for Identity
in the Fiction of

HENRY

JAMES

PHILIP SICKER

Love and
the Quest for Identity
in the Fiction of

HENRY
JAMES

PRINCETON UNIVERSITY PRESS

For Becky

Man is nothing till he is united to an image.
W.B. YEATS

Can we only love
Something created by our own imagination?
Are we all in fact unloving and unlovable?
Then one is alone, and if one is alone
Then the lover and beloved are equally unreal,
And the dreamer is no more real than his dreams.
T.S. ELIOT

So now I want, above all things
to preserve my nakedness
from the gibe of image-making love.
D.H. LAWRENCE

CONTENTS

ACKNOWLEDGMENTS

HENRY JAMES once wrote to a friend that he was interested only in that which was difficult; anyone who undertakes a study of James' fiction must share this fascination. There are several people who have made my task of writing easier and more fulfilling. Professors Robert Langbaum, J. C. Levenson, and Harold Kolb of the University of Virginia have each helped me to deepen the scope of my study and to understand more clearly James' place in nineteenth- and twentieth-century intellectual history. In a more personal way, I am indebted to Richard Glatzer, who shares my love for James and has been both my toughest critic and closest friend during every phase of research, writing, and revision. I would never have reached any of these stages without the sustained support of my parents. Their financial assistance enabled me to undertake this project while I was in graduate school, and their interest and enthusiasm have made the writing worthwhile. Finally, I owe a special thanks to Becky Cross, a debt that the following pages can only hope to repay. It was she who inspired the germinal idea of this book by helping me to discover that love is the essential key to unlocking the mysteries of our identity.

OUR general critical estimate of Henry James' works has risen dramatically during the past forty years, and the outflow of books and articles has swollen to oceanic proportions. Yet, in the rising tide of full-length studies of James' fiction—studies that cover every subject from his "fictional children" to his relation to Ibsen to his use of melodrama—not one has been predominately devoted to James' evolving conception of romantic love. Much energy *has* been expended in an attempt to account for the alleged absence of sexual passion in his work through speculations about his personal life. Rebecca West, in her short, provocative study of 1916, traces James' failure to inject passion into his novels—and all his other failures, as well—to his inability to serve in the Civil War. Her biographical approach to his works anticipates *The Pilgrimage of Henry James* by Van Wyck Brooks, who insists that James' decision to live in Europe alienated him from his native "sacred fount" of inspiration and feeling. James, Brooks implies, was unable to establish convincing emotional relationships in most of his mature works "because he lost his instinctive judgment of men and things."[1]

Since the 1930s, there has been wild critical surmise about James' possible sexual aberration; at various times he has been branded as homosexual, impotent, castrated, and sexually under-developed. It is hardly surprising that, during this period, *The Turn of the Screw* has all but replaced *Hamlet* as the favorite of Freudian critics. The most vicious and well-known assault on James' private life comes from Maxwell Geismar, who unabashedly calls James "a study in pure egotism" and claims that his failure either to marry or to write about sex resulted from his "infantile-pubescent . . . thwarted sexuality."[2] Incapable of mature physical love, he argues, James turned to narcissism (expressed in his late style) and chose as his major theme "the cash nexus." Geismar's judgments are far too vindictive, prejudiced, and speculative to command serious attention, but one pauses to wonder why a critic would devote 400 pages to the denigration of a major writer. In the light of much lurid speculation about James' sex life, James Thurber's compassionate explanation seems both plausible and refreshing: "[James] chose a loveless life because of his transfiguring conviction that the high art he practiced was not consonant with marriage, but demanded the monastic disciplines of chastity. He loved vicariously, though, and no man more intensely and sensitively."[3] West's, Brooks', and Geismar's books are paradigmatic of a common type of Jamesian criticism that wrongly assumes that the writer's personal experience with love and fictional conception of it throughout his career are identical. As I hope to show, James' vision of love, which begins as imaginary infatuation in the early tales, evolves in the final novels to a mystical union of body and spirit that is quite beyond anything he, or almost anyone else, could have derived from firsthand experience.

Jamesian criticism is fortunate in having two books that sanely and sensitively treat the love James knew in his life: *Henry James: The Major Phase* (1944), by F. O. Matthiessen, and Leon Edel's *Henry James: The Untried Years* (1953). Matthiessen beautifully clarifies James' delicate relation to Minny Temple, while Edel has checked the flow of a good deal of prurient criticism by convincingly locating the novelist's "obscure hurt" in his back.

Exclusive of biographical studies, there has been little progress made in the exploration of James' treatment of love until fairly recently. Most estimates come in books or articles that are primarily concerned with some other Jamesian theme; they range from Quentin Anderson's improbable contention that James, "our domestic Dante," inherited his Swedenborgian father's ideal of love and used it as the basis of a religious allegory stressing the redemptive power of marriage, to Ronald Wallace's high fanciful comparison of "the structure of love" in *The Golden Bowl* to that in *A Midsummer Night's Dream*. Only in the past dozen years or so has criticism shown signs of reevaluating James as a novelist of love. Naomi Lebowitz's *The Imagination of Loving* (1965), the most extensive study of the subject to date, is really more about James' conception of the morality of "relationship" than about his changing conception of romantic love. Lebowitz argues that James saw moral love as a full "commitment" to the flux of experience[4] and draws useful, and long overdue, comparisons between James and D. H. Lawrence. Closely related to Lebowitz's work is Lisa Appignanesi's long essay "Henry James: Femininity and Moral Sensibility" in her book *Femininity and the Creative Imagination* (1973). Beginning with Philip Rahv's observation that James, "estranged from typical masculine interests," treated love in "the finer female sense," she argues for a Jungian male/female bifurcation in his characters.[5] With Lebowitz, she holds that successful love relationships in James require the acceptance of flux—an acceptance of which only the "fluid, inward-looking female sensibility" is capable. Martha Banta, arguing along similar lines in *Henry James and the Occult* (1972), traces this psychosexual dichotomy to the influence of William James' psychical research. Going a step beyond both Lebowitz and Appignanesi, she connects feminine sensitivity in love to telepathy.[6]

Although these three studies have provided useful groundwork for portions of my own, none has attempted to trace the long and complex evolution of James' vision of romantic love through his fiction. More important, in stressing the unconscious nature of his characters, they have failed to consider the vital relationship between love and the conscious quest for identity—a quest that lies at the center of all of his major novels. The chapters that follow will investigate the psychological assumptions that led James to view romantic love as a means of giving shape to the self and will explore the way in which his conceptions of love and identity developed together during his career.

March 1979

Love and
the Quest for Identity
in the Fiction of
HENRY
JAMES

ONE

The Great Relation: James as
a Novelist of Love

IN HER autobiography, *A Backward Glance*, Edith Wharton remembers breathlessly preparing for her first evening in the presence of Henry James. The famous novelist was forty-five at the time, and his young admirer sought to gain his attention by arriving at dinner in a stunning Doucet gown. "I can see the dress still," she writes, "and it *was* pretty; a tea rose pink, embroidered with iridescent beads. But, alas, it neither gave me courage to speak, nor attracted the attention of the great man. The evening was a failure, and I went home humbled and discouraged." A year or two later in Venice a similar opportunity arose.

> Once more I thought: How can I make myself pretty enough for him to notice me? Well—this time I had a new hat; a beautiful new hat! I was almost sure it was becoming, and I felt that if he would only tell me so I might at last pluck up my courage to blurt out my admiration for "Daisy Miller" and *The Portrait of a Lady*. But he noticed neither the hat nor its wearer—and the second of our meetings fell as flat as the first. When I spoke to him of them years afterward he could not even remember having seen me on either occasion.[1]

Wharton's story amuses us because it seems so delightfully typical of the James whom three generations of readers have come to imagine: a stately, stuffy, fastidious man, too intellectually self-absorbed to ever fix his eye on a pretty girl, too effeminate and reserved to feel the stir of romantic attraction. Wharton's anecdotes, along with numerous others, have become part of a literary legend; they have been as separate brushstrokes in our popular portrait of "the Master."[2] It is an image that seems perfectly embodied in Max Beerbohm's cartoons of a portly, pigeon-breasted James with a drooping jowl, deep-set eyes, and an immense cranium. Regrettably, our impression of James the man has come to color our reading of his work. Like the artist-narrator of one of James' most celebrated stories, many readers have mistaken the common caricature for "the real thing."

Asked to name those novelists for whom love was a predominant theme, most of us would list the Brontës and Stendhal, Flaubert, George Sand and Proust, Hardy, perhaps, and, certainly, D. H. Lawrence. The English novel has never shown that obsession with matters of the heart that distinguishes its French counterpart, but Henry James, more than any other novelist writing in English with the exception of Lawrence, devoted his fiction to the study of romantic love. The statement will surprise those who know James only as a "difficult" writer concerned with the baroque intricacies of style and form, or as a super-subtle psychologist of the mannered upper class, comfortable only in the "museum world" of palazzos, galleries, and burnished drawing rooms. It is not merely the legend of James' life, however, that has given rise to the widely held, but unfounded, belief that he knew and cared little about love; more detrimental, finally, have been those scores of critics who, defining romantic love within the narrowest limits, have labeled him "passionless." As Leon Edel has observed, James is frequently victimized by people who talk about him without really having read him.[3] Such critics are fond of noting that Isabel Archer recoils from Goodwood's famous "white lightning" kiss at the end of *The Portrait of a Lady*, and that the heroine of "The Beast in the Jungle" dies without ever declaring a love she has harbored for her entire adult life. In defending James, it is easy to point out that his last three novels are all built around extramarital love affairs, but he always conceived of passion as something more than sexual encounters and romantic declarations. During his entire career, however, James was to labor under the charge of being emotionally frigid.

William James, Henry's first critic, foresaw the objection that countless others would voice when he wrote: "Of the people who experience a personal dislike, so to speak, of your stories, the most I think will be repelled by . . . something cold, thin-blooded and priggish suddenly popping in and freezing the genial current."[4] William himself felt "something of a want of blood" in his brother's tales, especially those in which Henry treated love. Writing to Henry in 1868 about "The Story of a Masterpiece," "one of those male vs. female subjects you have so often treated," he complains of "a want of heartiness or unction."[5] The first reviewers of James' fiction fulfilled William's prediction in much the same language he had used. The anonymous reviewer of "Madame de Mauves," writing in 1875, doubts "whether Mr. James has not too habitually addressed himself less to men and women in their mere humanity, than to a certain kind of cultivated people, who . . . are often a little narrow in their sympathies and poverty-stricken in the simple emotions."[6] The review had been generally favorable, but even those critics who praised James for the precision and psychological subtlety with which he sketched his characters could regret that their "wonderfully told vicissitudes of feeling leave us cold."[7] A reviewer of *Roderick Hudson* in 1876 commends the novel as "beautiful, powerful, tragical," but echoes a common complaint when she concludes "all it lacks is to have been told with more human feeling."[8] Following the lead of the satirist W. H. Mallock, a commentator in 1879 notes that to read *The American* is to be "intellectually tickled." Not only is the book weak "in sensuous imagery," but James himself "is so 'spirituel' . . . that he has not *sense* enough to give [his characters] form, still less flesh."[9]

It is not easy to determine exactly what these early critics had in mind in calling for "warmth," "simple emotions," "feeling," and "flesh." Their vagueness stems in part, perhaps, from a characteristic Victorian reluctance to speak directly about sex; such, at least, is the natural assumption today, in an age when romantic love has come to mean erotic love. It is more probable, however, that James' first reviewers were objecting to an absence, not of "fleshliness," but of traditional sentimentality. Most of them were part of a reading public that was addicted to Louisa May Al-

CHAPTER ONE

cott's happy-ending tales of domestic romance, the exotic mystery novels of Harriet Prescott, and the melodramatic propaganda of "realists" like Rebecca Harding Davis. James was not averse to sentiment insofar as it contributed to the "felt life" of a work, but, even as a twenty-two-year-old reviewer, he realized that emotional self-indulgence was the easiest way to ruin a story. The writer, he felt, had to use his imagination to feel fully the passions of his characters, yet he had also to stand beyond those passions, master them, hold them up to scrutiny. In a review of 1865, he writes: "A story based upon those elemental passions in which we seek the true and final manifestations of character must be told in a spirit of intellectual superiority to those passions. That is, the author must understand what he is talking about."[10] Few readers in 1865 or thereafter would grant that James himself sought truth in "elemental passions" or that he knew what he was talking about when he wrote about love. Even a more sophisticated audience whose notions of the love story were fed by novels as diverse as *Amelia, The Vicar of Wakefield, Waverley, Jane Eyre, Adam Bede*, and *The Last Chronicle of Barset* found James "unromantic." An early reviewer of *The Portrait of a Lady*, comparing James' novel to those of "the picturesque . . . poetical" Walter Scott, expresses the dissatisfaction of many readers when he notes that, although the novel is "full of love scenes and motives, more or less complex, we hardly remember a book of so little sentiment, at least of the effusive and old-fashioned kind."[11]

James' stories and novels are seldom traditionally "picturesque." He sets his characters down, neither in Scottish castles, nor on windswept moors, nor in the village green, but in libraries, salons, and formal gardens. Similarly, his early heroes are neither dashing country gentlemen nor strapping rustic lads full of simple emotions, but shy, self-effacing men like Poor Richard and Winterbourne, disturbed artists and invalids. Unlike those "old English writers" who "loved to tell of gentle milkmaids and girls that tended flocks,"[12] James' heroines distinguish themselves more frequently by their wit than by their beauty or simplicity. A critic of *The Europeans* voices a typical objection when he complains that "it is not easy to take a very romantic interest in a young person [Gertrude Wentworth] who 'was tall and pale, thin and a little awkward; her hair was fair and perfectly straight; her eyes were dark and they had the singularity of seeming at once dull and restless.' . . . "[13] Readers in 1880 might well puzzle over tales of love in which kisses take place offstage, tears are shed only in moderation, and violent fits of rage and jealousy are virtually unknown.

While a reviewer in 1881 could call this new treatment of love "realistic," he was incorrect in calling *The Portrait of a Lady* the "portrait of an age."[14] Other important writers during the last two decades of the nineteenth century were also rebelling against the tepid sentimentality of the Victorian tradition, but they were far from content with James' "realism." If James' Victorian reviewers had been reluctant to insist upon sexuality in the portrayal of love, writers like George Moore and H. G. Wells were not. Although Wells' attack on James is the more famous, Moore's is more virulent. The writer who could declare, "I invented adultery"— meaning that he had liberated the English novel from prurience— could also label James "the eunuch."[15] Actually, Moore's fascination with James' personal life was an early instance of a critical prurience from which James himself has yet to be liberated. In his *Confessions of a Young Man* (1886), Moore writes:

> The interviewer in us would like to ask Henry James why he never married; but it would be vain to ask, so much does he write like a man to whom all action is repugnant. He confesses himself on every page . . . James is a prude and Howells is the happy father of a numerous family; the sun is shining, the boys and girls are playing on the lawn, they come trooping in to high tea, and there is dancing in the evening.[16]

Wells' parodistic assault in *Boon*, published only a year before James' death, is essentially an expanded and slightly more refined version of Moore's criticism. "He didn't marry," writes Wells, "he didn't go upon adventures; lust, avarice, ambition, all these things that as Milton says are to be got 'not without dust and heat' were not for him. Blood and dust and heat—he ruled them out."[17] As a result, James' characters are all "eviscerated" and "denuded"; they can "never make lusty love, never go to angry war, never shout at an election or perspire at poker."[18]

Wells and Moore were by no means alone in their disapproval. Arnold Bennett, complaining of "a very considerable absence of passionate feeling," claims to have quit reading *The Ambassadors* on page 150.[19] Bennett, nevertheless, progressed considerably farther than Mark Twain, who wrote that James and his kind "analyzed the guts out" of feelings and later declared, in a letter to Howells, "As for *The Bostonians*, I would rather be damned to John Bunyan's heaven than read that."[20] By the 1890s, James found himself attacked on two fronts; while popular audiences were clamoring for "effusive emotions" and old-fashioned love plots, advocates of naturalism and turn of the century aesthetes were demanding the frank portrayal of erotic passion. Oscar Wilde, a chief representative of this latter group, thought *The Turn of the Screw* "a most wonderful, lurid, poisonous, little tale"; "James is developing," he wrote, "but he will never arrive at a passion, I fear."[21] Even after the turn of the century, when he had published a trio of novels that dealt with sexual desire and adultery more directly than any he had written before, his works were still considered squeamish and emasculate. Critics like F. M. Colby accused James of avoiding passion through an elaborate, circumlocutory style that was "his sufficient fig-leaf." "His love affairs," wrote Colby, "illicit though they be, are so stripped to their motives that they seem no more enticing than a diagram."[22] It is a judgment that has been echoed by numerous critics and novelists in more recent times. Rebecca West, in her pioneering study of James, scolded Isabel Archer for marrying without "the consciousness of passion"[23] and pronounced the love affairs in *The Sacred Fount* "not more interesting among these vacuous people than . . . among sparrows."[24] André Gide showed a similar penchant for avian metaphor in describing James' lovers as "winged busts . . . all the weight of the flesh is absent, all the shaggy tangled undergrowth, all the wild darkness."[25]

More telling, perhaps, than any single criticism is the indifference of Thomas Hardy and D. H. Lawrence, the only two English
novelists writing during James' career who explored love with a
seriousness comparable to his own.[26] In his own fashion, however,
James was no less a rebel against the treatment of love in Anglo-
American fiction than Hardy, no less concerned with human passion than Lawrence. From his earliest reviews of the 1860s, much
of James' literary criticism is a crusade against the very "blood-
lessness" and lack of passion of which he was so often accused.
Ironically, the novelist whom Moore would call "eunuch" applied
the same label to many of his peers in a letter of 1881: "You say
that literature is going down in the U.S.A. I quite agree with
you—the stuff that is sent me seems to me written by eunuchs and
sempstresses. But I think it is the same every where—in France &
in England."[27] Later, in the first years of the twentieth century,
when critics were still deriding the lack of sexual passion in his
works, the novelist whom Edith Wharton once called the most
"unshockable" person she knew was laboring to render the subject
of adultery suitable for the timorous editors of magazines like *Atlantic* and *Scribner's*. In his notes outlining the scheme for *The
Golden Bowl*, he writes: "Everything about it qualifies it for
Harper except the subject—or rather, I mean, except the adul-
terine element in the subject. But may it not be simply a question
of handling that? For God's sake let me try."[28]

More than any other writer of his generation, James wished to
atone for the "tremendous omission" in the English novel, which
he termed "the great relation between men and women, the constant world-renewal."[29] With a few exceptions, English writers
had explored man's "relations with the pistol, the pirate, the
police, the wild and tame beast"—every relation but the all-
important relation of love.[30] Although James' insatiable interest in
the ever-changing human scene led him to survey life both from
the balconies of Venetian palaces and from the doorways of London tenements, he unfailingly turned to love as the subject for his
art. From Roderick Hudson to Lambert Strether, and from Daisy
Miller to Maggie Verver, the thing that James' heroes and

heroines continually "do" is fall in love. Indeed, for certain characters in James' fictional universe—Ralph Touchett, May Bartram, and Alice Staverton, for example—loving becomes a solitary lifelong occupation. To understand James' spiritual values and his conception of human nature at its highest is to understand why he channeled so much of his creative energy into the portrayal of love. If James finds loving to be a calling sufficient unto itself, it is because he views it as the purest and most intense expression of man's capacity to feel life. Not infrequently in James' novels, loving becomes a virtual definition of "living." It is Ralph's love for Isabel alone that prolongs his life; it is Strether's fascination with Madame de Vionnet that inspires his impassioned advice of "live, live all you can"; and, when the fatally stricken Milly Theale declares that she wants so "to live," it is of Merton Densher she is thinking.

In James' mature work, the act of falling in love engages the total human "consciousness" in a way no other experience can. It animates the powers of discernment, memory, and intuition, immersing us fully in "the fountain of being." Since James judged the beauty and morality of art according to the "amount of felt life" that it conveyed,[31] he chose love as his subject in order to explore man at his highest pitch of "consciousness," at his most refined level of imaginative energy. Above all, the ideal of romantic love was so central to James' vision of the universe that he saw it not simply as the theme that could give form to his novels, but as the relation that gave form to human life itself. So essential to individual identity was the act of loving for James that he could speak of "man's relation with himself, that is with woman."[32] The quest for love throughout the length and breadth of James' fiction is, more than anything else, a continual quest for identity in a universe that seems to deny both permanent, objective values and the integrity of the self.

This conception of love as the central organizing principle in life was, in large part, an outgrowth of James' own experience. From his early childhood, it was his natural habit of mind to conceive of life, at its most intense, as a continuing drama; the only thing that his imagination required to transform a situation into a "scene" was the presence of a heroine. Upon the stage of James' life, as well as that of his fiction, his beloved cousin Mary [Minny] Temple remained "ever the heroine of the scene."[33] Recalling a summer vacation he spent with Minny in *Notes of a Son and Brother*, he speaks of their circle of friends as actors in the drama of his imagination. "If drama we could indeed feel this as being, I hasten to add, we owed it most of all to our just having such a heroine that everything else inevitable came. Mary Temple was beautifully and indescribably *that*. . . ."[34] Through no effort of her own, "everything that took place around her took place as if in primary relation to her and in her interest: that is, in the interest of drawing her out and displaying her the more."[35] Clearly, it was not Minny so much as James' imagination acting upon Minny that organized his experience around her. An act of such imaginative consecration could only be the sign of a profound love, and, to a great extent, James' undying love for Minny was the "primary relation" of his life.

The nature of James' relationship with his cousin has long been a source of perfervid, and often misguided, speculation among scholars. When James spent his memorable August with Minny in the White Mountains, she was a slender girl of twenty, two years younger than Henry. Like many of the heroines whom James modeled upon her, she was a fascinating, restless bundle of contradictions. She had a natural gaiety, "a lightness all her own," yet was "inconsequently grave at the core"; she burned with "a fine reckless impatience," yet she persistently strove to draw out "the play of life in others"; she was youthful innocence itself, yet "absolutely afraid of nothing she might come to by living with enough sincerity and enough wonder";[36] she was at once independent and gregarious, flirtatious and solemn, tragic and pathetic. In conversation, she was witty, impertinent, penetrating, and full of questions. In the ballrooms of Newport, she whirled before James' eyes in the arms of young men in uniform, crossing the floor with "long, light and yet almost sliding steps."[37] After

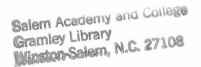

her death from tuberculosis at twenty-four, James wrote that "life claimed her and used her and beset her—made her range in her groping, her naturally immature and unlighted way from end to end of the scale. . . . "[38] To the young James, she seemed a radiant fountain of physical and mental energy, the quintessential embodiment of "conscious" life. Later, in the mind of the novelist, she was to become something nearly akin to that shimmering woman of Yeats' imagination, "a disengaged and dancing flame of thought."[39] Diffident and inexperienced in love, James could but worship Minny from afar during her lifetime; only after her death could she be captured, preserved in his memory, and reborn in his art.

Did James secretly hunger for a full-bodied romantic relationship with Minny? Would his adoring friendship have blossomed into a declaration of love had she lived? Was the novelist's eventual decision not to marry brought on by his frustrated love for his cousin? What are we to make of James' remark, in a letter to William, that he wished to regain his "natural lead" with Minny that his friendship might become "more active and masculine"?[40] Such questions ultimately lie in the province of the biographer, not the critic; the concern here is with the conception of love that James developed in his fiction, not with the love that he expressed during his life. For this purpose, Leon Edel's assessment of James' relationship with Minny will suffice: "We might say that Henry loved Minny as much as he was capable of loving any woman, as much as Winterbourne, uncertain and doubting in his frosty bewilderment, loved Daisy, or the invalid Ralph loved Isabel: a questioning love, unvoiced and unavowed, and not fully fathomed."[41] The question that remains for the critic—and it is a considerable one—is how much James' feeling for Minny shaped his ideas about love in his early work. Stated more precisely, did James' early portrayal of love as an image worshiped in the mind derive directly from his experience with Minny, or was his love for her the inchoate expression of a vision of love that had already begun to develop in his consciousness? The answer is not so clear-cut as this phraseology implies. James' first extended contact with Minny

came in the summer of 1865, and she died on March 8, 1870; the
years that intervene are those in which James, the voracious
reader, began testing his wings as a storywriter. Like all young
writers, James' aesthetic concerns took the hue of his emotional
experience, but they were also unmistakably colored by a temperament that was naturally reserved, delicate, and refined.

The picture of the adolescent James that emerges from his auto-
biographical writings is of a shy, brooding youth gazing rather de-
spondently from a darkened corner at his older brother cavorting
in the spotlight. In *Notes of a Son and Brother*, for example,
James recalls arriving at Harvard only "to find my brother on the
scene and already in a stage of progression upon its contents that I
resigned in advance never to reach . . . I seemed to feel a sort of
quickening savoury meal in any cold scrap of his own experience
he might let pass on to my palate."[42] In terms of experience, William seemed "always round the corner and out of sight, coming
back into view only at his hours of extremest ease," while Henry
"hung inveterately and woefully back."[43] From his earliest years,
long before Minny entered his life, James was an observer in life as
he would be in love, an expert in the art of resignation and self-
denial. Recalling the freedom that he enjoyed as a child, he concludes that "my infant license can only have had for its ground
some timely conviction on the part of my elders that the only form
of riot or revel ever known to me would be that of the visiting
mind."[44] James' natural proclivity for observing life from a distance became, to some measure, a necessary way of life after he
suffered a serious back injury in 1861. This mishap only served to
fulfill the young man's prophetic belief that he was "foredoomed"
to be one "in whom contemplation takes so much the place of
action."[45]

James' fascination with images also began before his first love.
In fact, his earliest childhood memory was imagined as a picture—a glimpse of the Place Vendôme "framed by the clear window" of a moving carriage.[46] More frequently, the images that he
preserved in his memory were of beautiful women, either etched,
painted, or in elaborate costume on stage. The child who had pored

over Thackeray's sketches of Becky Sharp and spent Sunday after-
noons paging through steel-plated volumes of pictures "devoted
mainly to the heroines of Romance,"[47] would, in later years, view
with the same fascination Raphael's radiant "Madonna of the
Chair," Bronzino's pale, haunting portrait of Lucrezia, and the
dark-eyed, melancholy beauties of Rossetti.[48] James' youthful
literary tastes further reflect his natural tendency to view life in
terms of caught images. One of his earliest preferences was for
romantic allegory—particularly the tales of Hawthorne and
Mérimée—in which people and ideas were transformed into symbols and brought forth like the luminous images in a stained glass
window. Mérimée's "La Venus d'Ille," which James first read as a
teenager, held a particular enchantment. So enthralled was he by
this tale of fatal love between a man and a statue of Venus that he
translated it and tried to publish it in a New York weekly. Not surprisingly, however, the images of women that James loved most
were those he beheld framed on a curtained stage. To read his re-
collections of the actresses whom he saw in his adolescence is like
turning the pages of an old volume of theater portraits. He recalls
Madame Celeste as "Miami the Huntress," her "wonderful majes-
tic and yet voluptuous stride enhanced by a short kilt, black velvet
leggings and a gun haughtily borne on the shoulder"[49]; Miss
Emily Mestayer "as the Eliza of Uncle Tom's Cabin, her swelling
bust encased in a neat cotton gown," making "her flight across the
ice-blocks of the Ohio"[50]; and the charming dark-haired heroine
of Le Père de la Débutante "in flowing white classically relieved by
a gold tiara and a golden scarf."[51]

As James indicates in A Small Boy and Others, he was not beyond harboring youthful infatuations for the actresses he watched,
nor for paying them "an homage quite other than critical." He
claims, in fact, that "the histrionic character" was first revealed to
him through his romantic attraction to two "strange, pale little
flowers of American theatre" called "the Boon Children," whom
he saw in person on a boat. Their "melancholy grace," "peevish
refinement," and general attitude of indifference filled him "with
fascination and yet with fear."[52] In life, James would always ap-

proach love with a mixture of "fascination" and "fear," and it was the combination of these impulses that, while rendering him susceptible to love, compelled him to love from a distance. All of this is not to minimize Minny Temple's influence on James' early fiction, but to suggest that the shy, ardent heroes of these stories, who worship at the altar of an idealized woman, are the inevitable embodiments of their creator's temperament. Minny provided James, not with an enduring vision of love—for that vision was to change radically during his career—but rather with a series of feminine portraits for his fiction. In her fleet grace and "ethereal brightness," she became the virgin huntress of the early tales; in her vivacious immaturity and innocence, she became "the American girl," Daisy Miller; in her piercing intelligence, thirst for experience, and "moral spontaneity," she became Isabel Archer; and, finally, in the tragic beauty of her death, she became Milly Theale. As James matured as an artist, his vision of love evolved far beyond the kind of image worship that he was prone to in his life, until it came to embody sexual and spiritual unification rather than idealization and detachment. Nevertheless, his natural inclination toward chastity and the worship of feminine beauty for its own sake led him, early in his career, to treat love as it had never before been treated in English fiction.

The Romantic movement that both popularized and despiritualized the ideal of courtly love in French and German fiction had little impact upon the English novel. When Romanticism was taking hold on the continent during the 1770s and 1780s, and German youths were re-enacting the suicide of the inconsolably passionate Werther, English readers were chuckling at the vagaries of Yorick and Uncle Toby Shandy. Over forty years later, when Stendhal, the last important novelist of the Romantic tradition, was composing his psychological treatise *De l'amour*, England's most popular novelist was writing Highland adventures. There had been a great deal of sentiment embodied in the English novel tradition before James, but mature, passionate love was almost unknown. Surveying the historical development of English fiction at the end of his

CHAPTER ONE

career, James could complain that from Fielding "straight down through all the Victorian time," English novelists had labored under "the fond superstition that the key . . . of each and every situation that could turn up for the novelist, was the sentimental key."[53] Frequently, English novelists skirted the question of romantic love altogether, and, when they treated it at all, they generally presented it in a radically reductive fashion: either as a social phenomenon revealing the manners and values of a particular class, eventuating in marriage and so many thousand pounds a year, or as a matter of mere sensual delight. There are, of course, two striking exceptions to this rule—*Wuthering Heights* and *Jane Eyre*. The Brontës, however, who imagined love as a mystical merging of two souls, are part of a tradition that begins with Plato and includes Dante, Donne, Goethe, Shelley, and Walt Whitman, and they stand completely outside the mainstream of the English novel. Samuel Richardson and Jane Austen had also portrayed love with psychological maturity—but it was a maturity to which James remained strangely insensitive. From the beginning, James thought the author of *Clarissa* woefully dispassionate and, although he took delight in Austen's "little strokes of human truth," he found in her work no penetrating truth about the human heart. In a 1905 essay, "The Lesson of Balzac," he mocks the delicacy that made "our dear, everybody's dear Jane" so popular with the timid publishers of the day, "so amenable to pretty reproduction in every variety of what is called tasteful." "Jane Austen," he writes, "with all her light felicity, leaves us hardly more curious of her process, or of the experience in her that fed it, than the brown thrush who tells his story from the garden bough."[54]

Although James' judgments overlook the psychological complexities of these writers, it is nonetheless true that neither Richardson nor Austen was predominantly concerned with the nature of love—with marriage, perhaps, but not with love. In their novels, as in those of Goldsmith, Thackeray, Dickens, and Trollope, love is always subservient to a social or economic interest. The famous opening sentence of *Pride and Prejudice* in many ways sums up this attitude toward male-female relationships: "It is universally acknowledged that a man in possession of a good fortune must be in want of a wife." The consuming interest is monetary and social, and the plot of this type of novel consists of the search for a marital partner who can satisfy that interest. The ramifications suggested by Austen's statement have filled scores of volumes. In every case, however, "love" is really a quest for status in a world of rigidly stratified classes. Richardson initiated this type of novel with *Pamela*, a servant girl who rises through virtue to wed her wealthy master; Austen gave us our most penetrating version of the quest in *Emma*; Thackeray exploited its comic possibilities in Becky Sharp's pursuit of Jos Sedley in *Vanity Fair*; Dickens turned it to mordant satire in Mr. and Mrs. Lammle of *Our Mutual Friend*, each of whom marries for money only to discover that the other is impoverished. Arnold Bennett, John Galsworthy, and, to a lesser degree, George Meredith carried on this tradition among writers of James' generation.

A second group of novelists, for whom relations between the sexes serve an erotic and comic end, includes such writers as Defoe, Fielding, Sterne, and Smollett. Not surprisingly, this attitude toward love is restricted almost exclusively to novelists of the eighteenth century and bears a closer resemblance to that found in Restoration drama than to anything in nineteenth-century English fiction. As in the plays of Etherege and Wycherley, "love" is primarily a sexual hunger, and our enjoyment in reading a novel like *Joseph Andrews* comes in watching the elaborate machinations through which characters like Lady Booby seek to gratify it. In his preface to Book Six of *Tom Jones*, Fielding notes that "what is commonly called love" is "the desire of satisfying a voracious appetite with a certain quantity of delicate, white female flesh." Although he rejects this definition, contending that true love "satisfies itself in a much more delicate manner," we tend to recall Tom's lusty encounters with Molly Seagrim, Mrs. Waters, and Lady Bellaston more than his quasi-spiritual union with Sophia at the end of the book. Similarly, although Defoe claims that Moll Flanders "always spoke with abhorrence of her former life," we marvel for several hundred pages at her insatiable carnal appetite and delight in her numerous bouts between the sheets. Smollett's Roderick Random and Peregrine Pickle sow their wild oats with abandon during the course of their adventures, while Sterne, fascinated by the sport of sexual attraction, ends *A Sentimental Journey* in mid-sentence as Yorick is about to seduce a chambermaid.

In both types of English novel, love is presented as a chase, and the goal, be it money or sex, is what compels our interest. In neither case is the intensity of the relationship nor the psychological course of its development the matter of primary concern; love is always a means to some other kind of fulfillment, both for the characters and for the reader. James, however, even in his earliest tales, views love not simply as a social convention or as a spasmodic impulse, but as a product of the imagination. Since the imagination in James' early fiction tends to idealize its beloved, and since the process of idealization thrives on distance and separation, there is almost never marriage or sexual union in these stories and novels. In James' recasting of the courtly conception of love, the emphasis shifts from the desire that is satisfied to that which is felt, from the end result of love to the process of its development.

From his earliest years as a writer, James was acutely aware of himself as a renegade from the Anglo-American tradition in his presentation of romantic love. Two centuries of English novelists, he felt, had fallen short in their treatment of adult life because, with emotional shallowness or Victorian reticence, they had failed to embrace man's "great relation." In James' view, these writers lacked the two essentials necessary for a mature depiction of love: passion and psychological insight. In an 1877 essay on George Sand, he sets forth this first objection: "Miss Austen and Sir Walter Scott, Dickens and Thackeray, Hawthorne and George Eliot have all represented young people in love with each other; but not one of them has, to the best of my recollection, described anything that can be called passion—put it into motion before us, and shown us its various paces."[55] Three years later, in reviewing Zola, James could write with acerbity, "our English system [of fiction writing] is a good thing for virgins and boys, and a bad thing for the novel itself. . . ."[56] Sand and Zola, James recognized, did present passion, but sexual desire is not the only form of passion, nor, James believed, is it the main ingredient in love. James states this belief most emphatically and eloquently in his review of modern Italian novelists in 1904. It is never the physical "passion of the hero and heroine that gives, that can ever give, the hero and heroine interest, but it is they themselves, with the ground they stand on and the objects enclosing them, who give interest to their passion." Unless the lovers possessed "something finely contributive in themselves," James felt that their relationship had no more interest nor dignity "than . . . the boots and shoes that we see, in the corridors of promiscuous hotels, standing often in double pairs at the doors of rooms."[57] The "passion" that James had in mind in his earliest reviews, and which he infused in his early stories and novels, has little to do with flaming kisses, heaving bosoms, or adulterous trysts in the forest; by "passion," James meant an inner fire of the imagination that is fed more by unsatisfied desire than by emotional fulfillment, more by hopelessness than by hope. It is a passion that has as its object not a woman of flesh and blood so much as the visionary image of a woman. "Imaginative passion," so defined, is essentially a religious sentiment, an adoration of consuming, sometimes incinerating, emotional intensity. Love, James realized, was not only the most intense of human experiences, but also the most complex; it involved not simply sexual desire, but creation, self-deception, and self-torture as well.

The analysis of these interior processes that make love vital and interesting was quite beyond the novelist who presented only the surface of life. The "great" novelist, James wrote in 1865, "must know *man* as well as *men*, and to know man is to be a philosopher."[58] It is also, one might add, to be a psychologist of human behavior. Richardson, Fielding, and Smollett had oversimplified man by being "emphatically preachers and moralists," and, with the exception of George Eliot, whose penetration he admired, James held that the novelists of his own century had presented little more than superficial "figures and pictures."[59] James was an early devotee of Scott and, in one of his first reviews, he praises the Scotsman's "vast and rich imagination." Since Shakespeare, no writer had created "so immense a gallery of portraits, nor, on the whole had any portraits been so lifelike."[60] At the same time, however, James realized that Scott was not a psychological novelist, but a storyteller, a "fireside chronicler," and that his triumphs, like those of a technically perfect portrait painter, were "triumphs of fact," of brilliant surface detail. Years later, in his preface to *The Princess Casamassima*, he diagnosed Scott's inability to portray a convincing love relationship ("the 'feeling' question") between Edgar and Lucy Ashton in *The Bride of Lammermoor* as a psychological shallowness in presentation. "Edgar of Ravenswood . . . has a black cloak and hat and feathers more than he has a mind; just as Hamlet, while equally sabled and draped and plumed, while at least equally romantic, has yet a mind still more than he has a costume."[61] James scarcely expected to find Hamlets gracing the novels of his own day, but he demanded characters who were more than merely "lifelike"; to understand love, he believed, one needed to explore man's buried life, the hidden wellspring of his ideas, fantasies, and passions. George Eliot came closest to revealing this life; she "was a thinker," James held, "not, perhaps, a passionate one, but at least a serious one; and the term can be applied with either adjective neither to Dickens nor Thackeray."[62] As a child, James had loved Dickens and, in his maturity, he thought him, like Scott, "a great observer and a great humorist." At the same time, he complained that Dickens "has created nothing but figure. He has added nothing to our understanding of human character."[63] James was less fond of Trollope, but he noted that he too "was an excellent, an admirable observer." Like the other writers of his age, however, he dealt "wholly in small effects." Detached from their social milieu and reduced "to their essences," his characters were "but halves of men and women."[64] Human beings, James insisted, were more than merely bundles of eccentricities, and love was more than tears and kisses or a quickening in the loins. Even as a novice storywriter, he realized that a "whole man" is defined not merely by the purple cravat he wears, the port he drinks at dinner, or the amount of gold he has stored away, but by the secretive, passionate desires that seethe and boil in his imagination.

TWO

A Sacred Terror: Love, Death, and Change in James' Early Fiction

Madone! my lady, I will build for thee
A grotto altar of my misery.
BAUDELAIRE

HENRY JAMES' lifelong treatment of love as a quest for identity grew directly out of his belief in the subjective nature of all experience. When James speaks of "the air of reality," he is referring, not to any fixed objective truth in the natural world, but to the stream of impressions that continually cascade through the individual consciousness. "If experience consists of impressions," he writes in "The Art of Fiction," "it may be said that impressions *are* experience, just as (have we not seen it?) they are the very air we breathe."[1] Each of these quickly dissolving impressions is utterly unique, James believed, because we perceive them not simply through our outer ocular vision, but with the transforming inner eye of memory and thought association. Each impression becomes an inextricable blend of past and present vision; each moment of experience is a multilayered temporal event permeated with the distinctive flavor of one's being. Starting with his earliest stories, James anticipated the theory of perception that his brother William put forward in his *Principles of Psychology* (1890): "Whilst part of what we perceive comes through our senses from the object before us, another part (and it may be the larger part) always comes . . . out of our own head."[2] We need not read far into James' work to find illustrations of this idea. The narrator of "A Passionate Pilgrim" (1871), for instance, sees an old English inn with the eyes of one who has seen it all before "in books, in visions, in dreams, in Dickens, in Smollett, and Boswell,"[3] the hero of "Travelling Companions" (1870) finds his impressions of Italy colored by his readings of Stendhal, and, as we shall see, nearly all of James' characters see their beloved through the prism of an imaginary ideal.

The "house of fiction" that the novelist describes in his preface to *The Portrait of a Lady* is really the house of life, from whose windows each occupant sees the world differently:

> The house of fiction has in short not one window, but a million—a number of possible windows not to be reckoned, rather; every one of which has been pierced, or is still pierceable, in its vast front, by the need of the individual vision and by the pressure of the individual will. These apertures, of dissimilar shape and size, hang so, all together, over the human scene that we might have expected of them a greater sameness of report than we find. They are but windows at the best, mere holes in a dead wall, disconnected, perched aloft; they are not hinged doors opening straight upon life. But they have this mark of their own that at each of them stands a figure with a pair of eyes, or at least with a field-glass, which forms, again and again, for observation, a unique instrument, insuring to the person making use of it an impression distinct from every other. He and his neighbors are watching the same show, but one seeing more where the other sees less, one seeing black where the other sees white, one seeing big where the other sees small, one seeing coarse where the other sees fine. And so on, and so on. . . .[4]

Not only does each person perceive a world different from anyone else's, but he sees as well one that is unique during every moment of experience. The individual viewer in James' "house" is not a fixed quantity, but an ever-changing summation "of what he has *been* conscious." Each momentary impression flashes in the subjective consciousness and then passes into the corridors of memory. In doing so, however, it infinitesimally alters the perceiving self by adding to the sum of what he has perceived. Since one's view of the world, from moment to moment, is determined by what one is—that is, the totality of what one has experienced— one never sees the same object the same way twice. We are, in James' metaphysics, slightly different people from one waking moment to the next.

The concept of subjectivism did not begin with James, of course.

Kant laid the psychological foundations for the Romantic movement—of which James is a descendant—before the beginning of
the nineteenth century, when he theorized that "reality" was relative to the shifting perspectives of the individual consciousness.
Working upon the same assumption, Wordsworth and Coleridge
celebrated the unique transforming power of the private mind,
which half perceives and half creates its own reality over and over
again. James, too, believed that each human consciousness carries
its own changing world; but, while the romantics had primarily
investigated the mind's transformations of the world around it,
James was acutely concerned with the transformations of the individual mind itself.

Among Victorian writers, he stands with Walter Pater at the
gateway of twentieth-century fiction in his realization that the
perceiver, as well as the reality he perceives, is unique and ever
changing. Like James', Pater's conception of personality begins
with the belief that each individual is isolated within the sphere of
his own consciousness. In his famous conclusion to *The Renaissance*, he speaks of "each mind keeping as a solitary prisoner its
own dream of a world," separated from every other mind "by that
thick wall of personality through which no real voice has ever
pierced on its way to us."[5] The "self," for both Pater and James, is
merely the sum of its experiences, and, because this experience is a
whirlpool of impressions, it follows that there can be no stable
source of identity within the conscious mind. As Graham Hough
has rightly observed, it is difficult to see where this kind of
atomized, solipsistic epistemology is leading in the realm of individual conduct.[6] Any personal code of behavior requires a conception of integrated selfhood—that is, a sense of one's personality
(or some aspect of it) continuing unchanged through time. But if
there is nothing permanent within either the self or the sphere of
its perceptions, and if each person is really locked within an airtight world of his own vision, then what becomes of personal identity? Unlike Pater, who considered this question only in *Marius
the Epicurean* (1885), James addressed it from the very outset of
his career. When, in 1873, Pater wrote of "the passage and disso-

lution of impressions, images, sensations . . . that continual van-
ishing away, that strange, perpetual weaving and unweaving of
ourselves,"[7] he unknowingly formulated the problem that Henry
James was wrestling with in his early tales.

Unlike many of his literary descendants who join with Joyce's
Stephen Dedalus in lamenting the continuous flux of audible and
visible experience, Pater could revel in the inextricable, ever-
proliferating life that surrounds the sensitive consciousness. His
only advice for living in this chaotic sea of impressions was to pass
"swiftly from point to point, and [to] be present where the
greatest number of vital forces unite in their purest energy." At
times, James seems to burn with this same hard, gemlike flame, to
relish experience for its own sake, as in "The Art of Fiction,"
where he describes "experience" as "a kind of huge spider-web of
the finest silken threads suspended in the chamber of consciousness, and catching every airborne particle in its tissue."[8] In his autobiography, the novelist recalls that, even in earliest childhood,
his paramount desire was "just to be somewhere—almost anywhere would do—and somehow feel an impression or an acces-
sion, feel a relation or a vibration."[9] Throughout his life, James
was instinctively attracted by Pater's cult of refined sensation, and
the hero of his first major novel, *Roderick Hudson* (1875), sounds
like a Paterean when he rapturously describes his sense of Italy:
"There are twenty moments a week—a day, for that matter, some
days—that seem supreme, twenty impressions that seem ultimate, that appear to form an intellectual era. But others come
treading on their heels and sweeping them along, and they all melt
like water into water. . . ."[10] Yet we would be wrong to read this
hyperbolic outburst without sensing the mature irony that informs it, for Roderick is one of the most childish protagonists
James ever created. Even in the early 1870s, the novelist realized
that there was something naive and futile about a life of cultivated
solipsism. In later years, he would mockingly characterize the
Oxford aesthetician as "a mask without a face" and compare his
gemlike flame to a "lucent matchbox."

James' early dislike of Impressionist painting was also a reaction against the formlessness of purely subjective experience. After viewing the 1876 exhibition at Durand-Ruel's, he declared that " 'Impressionist' doctrines" were "incompatible, in an artist's mind, with the existence of first-rate talent."[11] In a sense, painters such as Renoir, Monet, and Pissarro were trying to express on canvas the quality of experience that Pater had described in his conclusion. The works that James examined attempted to express the shifting, dancing play of light, water, and clouds as momentarily seen by the individual eye; inner and outer worlds were in constant metamorphosis. Although these assumptions about the impermanent, relativistic nature of reality were very close to James' own, he was appalled by the idea of merely recreating subjective chaos in art. In later years, his view of the Impressionists would mellow, but, in an 1876 dispatch to the New York *Tribune*, he spoke of them disparagingly as "absolute foes of arrangement, embellishment [and] selection . . . to give a vivid impression of how a thing happens to look, at a particular moment, is the essence of their mission."[12] James noted that this attitude had something in common with that of the Pre-Raphaelites, but his marked preference for Hunt, Rossetti, and Millais sprang from the fact that these artists longed to freeze a moment of individual perception in sharp, intricate detail, while the Impressionists wished to reveal the processes through which the mind perceives. James' lifelong insistence upon order in his own art was really a natural outgrowth of his desire to find a principle of order in the self. And, as he developed his fiction, he became increasingly aware of the individual's need to discover or create some coherent inner identity amid the ebb and flow of sensations. If there were no absolutes either in the physical universe or in the human psyche, he recognized that the exhilaration of heightened consciousness would inevitably degenerate into something akin to Henry Adams' chaotic sense of being a "limpet" adrift in a "supersensual ocean."

Nearly all of the protagonists whom James created during the first decade of his career feel lost within the unbounded prison of their own conscious minds. When Christina Light complains, "I am tired to death of myself; I would give all my possessions to get

out of myself,"[13] she echoes the feelings of a dozen male characters before her. These early figures are the most unheroic of
heroes; almost without exception, they are passive, dissipated,
bewildered, and mentally or physically debilitated. The twenty-six
tales that James composed before 1875 are peopled by a collection
of demented artists, chronic invalids, drunkards, suicides, ineffec-
tual dilettantes, and hypochondriacs. These afflicted people have in
common a sense of alienation both from the society around them
and from their own past. They are horrified at their isolation in a
self-enclosed world that whirls continually around them, and they
long for a source of permanence in their lives. "Who am I?" asks
the neurotic hero of "A Passionate Pilgrim"; "My name is Clement Searle. I was born in New York. What am I? I assure you,
nothing. . . . I'm a failure, sir. . . . Of what I was to begin with no
memory remains. I have been ebbing away from the start, in a
steady current which, at forty, has left this arid sand bank behind."[14]

The overwhelming question "Who am I?" informs all of James'
fiction, and, from the very beginning of his career, he realized that
love alone might provide the answer by allowing man to break out
of the disordered prison of his own mind. Nowhere is the importance of love more clearly suggested in his early work than in the
opening pages of *Roderick Hudson*. "I am tired of myself," Rowland Mallet complains to his cousin Cecilia, "my own thoughts,
my own affairs, my own eternal company. True happiness, we are
told, consists in getting out of one's self; but the point is not only
to get out—you must stay out; and to stay out you must have
some absorbing errand. . . . I want to care for something or for
somebody. And I want to care with a certain ardour, even, if you
can believe it, with a certain passion. I can't just now feel ardent
about a hospital or a dormitory. . . ." Cecilia's reply is unmistakably James' own: "What an immense number of words . . . to say
you want to fall in love."[15] This is, of course, precisely what Rowland proceeds to do. For James, love begins with the mind's belief
in the autonomy of a consciousness outside the self, a belief in the
stable otherness of another person. Only by focusing attention

upon something that seems fixed, beyond "the dusky, crowded, heterogeneous backshop of the mind," can the individual gain a sense of his own psychic permanence. The idea of an integrated self is, in short, possible only when we can see ourselves in perpetual relation to a fixed point; and, in order to seem fixed, this point—or "love-image," as I shall refer to it in the early tales—must appear to exist beyond the transient sphere of our own ego. I emphasize "seeming" and "believing" here because, given James' epistemology, we can never really escape the prison of self through ordinary modes of perception. As James painfully realized, to perceive anything consciously is to reduce it to a mere subjective impression, and to freeze the flow of these impressions in an image is to falsify experience. The beautiful maidens of his early tales are actually no less subject to change than the men who worship an imaginary conception of them. Although these early heroes devoutly believe that their love-images are real, they can achieve, at best, the illusion of a fixed relation. More frequently, they are driven to the unbearable discovery that the woman whom they have idealized bears no resemblance to her flesh and blood counterpart. Their quests for self-definition are foredoomed from the start because their love grows out of mere cognitive perception. James realized at the outset of his career that love could never liberate man from himself and place him in vital relation to another unless it originated in some deeper dimension of consciousness. In 1865, however, he could scarcely have said precisely what that other dimension might be; only in the novels that he wrote after the turn of the century do his characters discover a means of going beyond self-made images.

"The Story of a Masterpiece" (1868) is one of James' earliest attempts to analyze the process of self-deception through which one falls in love with an imaginary ideal. John Lennox, a wealthy, middle-aged widower, becomes engaged to a young American blonde named Marian Everett. We realize that Lennox is more enamored of something in Marian's outward appearance than of the girl herself when he becomes enchanted with the portrait that has been partly modeled upon her, of "a fair haired young woman, clad in rich medieval dress, and looking like a countess in the Renaissance" (1:263). When he commissions its creator, Stephen Baxter, to paint his fiancée again, we learn that the painter had also once loved Marian. With appropriate irony, he has entitled his original painting "My Last Duchess"; like the portrait of Browning's ill-fated duchess, Marian's portrait conceals more than it reveals about its subject. The Renaissance trappings endow the picture with an atmosphere of refinement and purity, but the subject wears "an expression so ambiguous that Lennox remained uncertain whether it was a portrait or a work of fancy." In truth, the portrait is largely fanciful—a visual representation, not of the real Marian, but of a perfected image of her with which both Baxter and Lennox have fallen in love.

Having failed in his suit years before, Baxter has learned that Marian, like her poetic counterpart, has "a heart too soon made glad." "My heart," she later tells her fiancé, "is the whole world. My heart's everywhere" (1:285). This magnanimous dispersion of sentiment, even if it is sincerely felt, makes intense personal love impossible, for to claim to love everyone is to be incapable of deeply loving anyone. Reviewing his impressions of Marian after she has deserted him, Baxter realizes that, beneath her "young loveliness and ariel grace," she is "irreclaimably light . . . hollow, trivial, vulgar" (1:279). He senses "something factitious and unreal in his fancied passion" for a little American poseur. Freed from his illusion, Baxter is able to paint Marian as she actually is, to reveal her character through a strict representation of physical details. "I go in for reality," he explains to Lennox in defending his mimetic, historically accurate composition:

It was Marian, in very truth, and Marian most patiently measured and observed . . . Nothing could be more simple than the conception and composition of the picture. The figure sat peacefully, looking slightly to the right, with head erect and hands—the virginal hands without rings or bracelets—lying idle on its knees. The blond hair was gathered into a little knot of braids on the top of the head (in the fashion of the moment) and left free the almost childish contour of ears and cheeks (1:283-284).

Whereas the first portrait had employed ornate costuming and a vagueness of expression to give the illusion of depth, the second, with its "deliberate" simplicity, reveals that depth to be an illusion. The emotional wisdom of the painter is expressed, paradoxically, through the shallowness of his subject. Stripped of her "ambiguity," Marian's likeness reveals to Lennox only a "horrible blankness and deadness." Gazing at the portrait, he discovers to his horror that "some strangely potent agent had won from his mistress the confession of her inmost soul, and written it there on the canvas in firm yet passionate lines. Marian's person was lightness—her charm was lightness" (1:285).

Like Stendhal before him, James realized that once a love-image is shattered, there is no sane way of mending it. Through his dual protagonists, he explored the two possible roads that consciousness can take in the moment of disillusionment: Baxter's painful but sobering recognition of his error in judgment and Lennox's frantic retreat in a realm of complete self-deception. Like James, Baxter gains a certain consolation through the creation of order and permanence in his art. Further, in transferring the burden of his disenchantment to the canvas, he frees himself from his obsession for Marian by presenting her in the transparent light of truth. To love only an image is to focus one's imaginative vision on a single frame on the cinematic reel of experience. In his first work, Baxter had merely transferred such an image to the canvas; in the second, "he had almost composed." In "The Story of a Masterpiece," James, the novice storyteller, suggested an all-important equation between love and art that he would elaborate in his more mature fiction: real love, like good art, is never a product of pure imagination, but an alchemic blend of imagination, acute observation, and sympathy. For Lennox, who loves pictures but cannot paint, art is the source of agony rather than solace. Unable to reaffirm his original vision of Marian by visibly reproducing it, he desperately seeks to deny the truth of Baxter's portrait. His vision of Marian as an eternal paragon of purity and refinement is so central to his conception of himself that to recognize the falsity of his love would be to recognize the falsity of his imagined identity. When he discovers that even the original picture that had crystallized his love-image has lost its charm, he irrationally seeks to efface his mature knowlege of Marian by destroying the artist's second work. Pronouncing the second Marian a "detestable creature I can neither love or respect," he thrusts a poignard "with barbarous glee, straight into the lovely face of the image" (1:295). Nearly thirty years later, Wilde's Dorian Grey, seeking to kill the image of his moral corruption in a similar gesture, would destroy himself. Lennox strives to kill the image of his own romantic blindness and so destroys his rational intelligence. By the end of the tale, his entire life has become a self-induced hallucination: "I need hardly add that on the following day Lennox was married" (1:296).

Although love drives many of James' early protagonists to madness, it drives very few to marriage. James Kraft points out that the original version of "The Story of a Masterpiece" made no mention of Lennox's nuptials, and that James added this ending only at the request of his publisher.[16] This is significant because the idealized love to which Jamesian heroes are addicted thrives, not upon psychological and emotional intimacy, but upon separation. James realized that we create love-images, not out of what we see, but out of what we fail to see, and his characters instinctively prefer to worship at a distance from their lover's altar. Theobald, the pathetic little artist in "The Madonna of the Future" is perhaps the purest and most idealistic of all these lovers. In his quest for permanence, he has sequestered himself in Florence, where the works of Michelangelo and Raphael endure "through the slow centuries in the gaze of an altered world" (3:21). Theobald's consuming ambition, the narrator soon discovers, is to paint the perfect madonna, to create for the modern world "that ineffable type [that] is one of the eternal needs of man's heart." Standing before "The Madonna of the Chair," he theorizes that Raphael saw her image, "not as a poet in five minutes' frenzy . . . but for days together . . . fixed, radiant, distinct, as we see it now" (3:20). After years of devoted observation, Theobald has evolved his own visionary madonna—a kind of composite of all the loveliest virgins ever painted. Unfortunately, the artist believes that this incandescent image has been miraculously incarnated in a real woman, "the beautiful Serafina."

Twenty years before meeting the narrator, Theobald had been enchanted by a young girl and had saved her from poverty and shame. Since then, he has kept her lodged in a high, dim chamber overlooking Florence, anticipating the day on which she will sit for his masterpiece. His entire life is a ritual performed in her honor: each night he climbs up to her apartment to admire her by twilight, each day he dreams of reproducing her image. Only when the narrator sees Serafina for himself does he realize "the immensity of [Theobald's] illusion; how, one by one, the noiseless years ebbed away, and left him brooding in charmed inaction, forever preparing for a work forever deferred" (3:37). While Theobald sees only the girl whom he met two decades earlier, time has transformed "the most beautiful woman in Italy" into the stout, middle-aged mistress of a charlatan sculptor. So inextricably is the artist's sense of self bound up with his vision of Serafina that, when the narrator declares she is old, he protests: "Old— old? . . . If she is old, what am I? If her beauty has faded, where—where is my strength? Has life been a dream? Have I worshipped too long, —have I loved too well?" (3:37) Unable to believe any longer in the fixed, external reality of his beloved, Theobald realizes that his own life has been but an ever-shifting illusion, that his identity is but as a reflection in a pool of water. He returns home feverishly to paint his madonna from memory, but, when the narrator visits him ten days later, he finds him sitting catatonically before "a canvas that was a mere dead blank, cracked and discolored by time" (3:47). Theobald berates himself as a failure, grows progressively weaker, and soon dies of brain fever. Once again, James suggests that love, like art, is doomed to failure if it exists only as an "idée fixe"; but the analogy that he invites us to draw between love and death is even more crucial to his vision of experience. To freeze an impression is to deaden the circuit of life, and, ultimately, to destroy one's capacity to think, respond, and create. Despite his fear of the chaos of private experience, James grew increasingly aware that flux is life itself, and that true permanence is found only in the grave. He realized that to define oneself as a fixed image reflected in the fixed image of a loved one is not simply to seek an illusion within an illusion, but to seek death itself. Theobald yearns for extinction only after his ideal is shattered—for many of the characters whom we shall consider shortly, love itself is a foretaste of death.

Henry James was not, of course, the first writer to portray love as an image worshiped in the mind. When Shakespeare wrote in *A Midsummer Night's Dream* that "the lunatic, the lover and the poet are of imagination all compact" he was drawing upon a tradition of courtly love that had entered Western literature five centuries earlier. Tracing the origins of this tradition to the ballads of twelfth-century Provence, Denis de Rougemont points out that the courtly lover does not love an actual woman, but rather a feminine ideal that crystallizes his dream of being in love.[17] According to Rougemont, this concept of image-love grew out of the Cathar religion, an heretical scion of Christianity that substituted passionate human love for divine love, or "agape," and that found its first artistic embodiment in the songs of the troubadours. The courtly ideal was given its purest expression in medieval romances and was later Christianized by Dante, secularized by the romantic poets, and psychologized by writers from Stendhal to Proust. What has remained constant throughout all these metamorphoses is the lover's habitual desire to maintain a distance between himself and the object of his adoration.[18] By so doing, he is able to keep his love-image perfect and unattainable and, thus, to heighten his intense imaginative longing. In many respects, the heroes of James' early tales are Victorian-age courtly lovers. Like the knights of twelfth-century French romances, they long for a beautiful but inaccessible woman, worship her from a self-imposed distance, and languish in a fatal lovesickness.

The women whom these Jamesian males adore are almost invariably compared to some image in the world of art, and they are figured forth as portraits, statues, and dramatis personae. In "The Story of a Year" (1865), for example, the first published tale to bear James' name, soldier John Ford marches off to war declaring that he will think of his fiancée, Lizzie, as do those "Catholics [who] keep little pictures of their adored Lady in their prayer books" (1:54). Returning home injured, he dies gazing upon her like "an old wounded Greek, who at falling dusk has crawled into a temple to die, steeping the last dull interval in idle admiration of sculptured Artemis" (1:96). Although James fails to explain why the pictured madonna is suddenly converted into a marble huntress, it seems clear that Ford takes comfort in imagining his lover transformed from the chaotic realm of life into the unchanging realm of art. In similar fashion, Robert Graham of "Osborne's Revenge" (1868) thinks of his beloved as " 'The White Lady' in *The Monastery*, who used to appear to the hero at the spring" (2:13); the protagonist of "Travelling Companions" (1870) fancies his lover's face on the Virgin Mary of an obscure Italian painting; Lennox sees his lover in the portrait of a duchess; Theobald imagines a Roman matron as a miraculous synthesis of all the best madonnas ever painted; and to Longmore's eye, the delicate beauty of Madame de Mauves (1874) "acquired . . . the serious cast of certain blank-browed Greek statues" (3:145). Count Valerio carries this obsession to its most perverse extreme in "The Last of the Valerii" (1874) by falling desperately in love with the statue of an ancient goddess itself. Although James' own natural proclivity for framing real-life impressions as imaginative pictures obviously contributed to this tendency in his characters, there was a group of painters and poets flourishing in England during the 1850s and 1860s who probably helped to shape the curious relationship between art and love in his early work. The Pre-Raphaelites, with their interest in things medieval, not only revivified the courtly view of love in their poetry, but characteristically cast their women as artistic images: snow white damozels framed against the golden bars of heaven, alabaster statues, portraits recalled from the past.

James had seen "the first fresh fruits of the Pre-Raphaelite efflorescence" as an adolescent in 1856. In *A Small Boy and Others*, he recalls that, "the very word Pre-Raphaelite wore for us that intensity of meaning, not less than of mystery, that thrills us in its perfection but for one season, the prime hour of first initiations. . . ."[19] What attracted James most to Pre-Raphaelite poetry and painting was its finely wrought precision, that scrupulous attention to color and detail that not only preserved a momentary impression, but endowed it with an intricate perfection of form. It is not surprising that a young writer who wished to construct his fictions around "the cherished scene" would be fascinated by a brotherhood of artists whose painters seemed to tell a story and whose poets strove to sketch a picture. Burne-Jones, James wrote in 1875, "paints, we may almost say, with a pen." Along with Rossetti, his pictures "always seem as if, to be complete, they needed to have a learned sonnet, of an explanatory sort, affixed to the frame. . . ."[20] As a poet, Rossetti's approach to language was remarkably similar to James' own; he wished to give words the hard, fixed arrangement of visual art, to arrest a moment of life in all its shimmering evanescence. Like Rossetti, James had longed to be a kind of painter-poet in his youth. The products of his adolescent imagination were short, dramatic pieces accompanied by a series of sketches, and, even near the end of his life, he could recall the manner of their composition:

> When the drama itself had covered three pages, the last one, over which I most labored, served for the illustration of what I had verbally presented . . . I thought, I lisped, at any rate, I composed, in scenes; though how much, or how far the scenes "came" is another affair . . . the animation of dialogue, the multiplication of designated characters, were things delightful in themselves—while I panted toward the canvas on which I should fling my figures; which it took me longer to fill than it had taken me to write what went with it. . . .[21]

The images that the Pre-Raphaelites most often wished to preserve were of beautiful women, and, when James visited Rossetti's studio in 1869, the portraits he saw struck a deep responsive chord.

Just as James had found in Minny Temple the image of feminine beauty that he was to embody in much of his fiction, Rossetti sought, over and over again, to capture Jane Morris on canvas. When James met Mrs. Morris shortly after his visit, he found himself envisioning her as a work of art, much in the manner of his early heroes. "Oh, ma cherie, such a wife," he wrote to his sister Alice.

> *Je n'en reviens pas*—she haunts me still. A figure cut out of a missal—out of one of Rossetti's or Hunt's pictures—to say this gives but a faint idea of her, because when such an image puts on flesh and blood, it is an apparition of fearful and wonderful intensity. It's hard to say whether she's a grand synthesis of all the pre-Raphaelite pictures ever made—or they a "keen analysis" of her—whether she's an original or a copy.[22]

In much the same way that Rossetti's paintings and Swinburne's poetry repeatedly pay homage to certain feminine archetypes, James' early tales are inspired by a particular ideal of womanhood—the virgin. Nearly every desirable female whom James created during the first decade of his career seems to her lover an incarnation either of Diana or Mary, and it is this, more than any other single factor, that makes his treatment of love in these tales so distinctive.

To love the image of a virgin is, of course, to love without hope or desire of consummation, for sexual fulfillment would destroy the very quality worshiped. What many of James' early heroes cherish is not the idea of a beautiful woman so much as the idea of their own suffering. They love from afar so as to increase their futile longing. In stories like "Poor Richard," "A Most Extraordinary Case," and "Longstaff's Marriage," James anticipates Proust and Mann by presenting love as self-induced disease that afflicts both the mind and body. The hero's sublime agony is possible only so long as the woman remains aloof, virginal, and perfect in his eyes. In order to stay in love, therefore, he must blind himself to everything in his beloved that does not correspond to this image.

Rougemont sums up the nature of image-love well when he writes: "Whatever turns into a reality is no longer love."[23] Most frequently in the early tales, the beloved is seen as a pale, icy Diana rather than as her warmer Christian counterpart. James' attraction to this figure in literature was long-standing, and his youthful reviews of the Pre-Raphaelites serve as fit companion pieces for many of his first tales. Reviewing Morris' *The Earthly Paradise* in 1868, he selected his three favorite legends for special comment: "Cupid and Psyche," "Atalanta's Race," and "Pygmalion and the Image." Significantly, each tale concerns the human love of a seemingly unattainable image or divinity. James greatly preferred Morris' "modesty of imagination" to Swinburne's eroticism and loved his "Atalanta" in particular. The "mild invincibility of [Morris'] heroine, and the half-boyish simplicity of her demeanor" made her "a perfect model of the 'belle inhumaine.' "[24] Perhaps this swift Greek huntress called to mind James' graceful, quick-striding cousin, Minny Temple, who had begun to acquire a kind of mythic stature in his eyes even during her lifetime. Whatever the source of the young writer's attraction, he created the first of a series of pale, elusive "belles inhumaines" in his fiction during the year in which he reviewed Morris.

In "A Most Extraordinary Case" (1868), Colonel Ferdinand Mason returns home from the chaos of the Civil War infirm and drained of his will to live. Mason's case is far from grave and, under his aunt's care, he shows definite signs of recovery—until he falls in love with his niece, Caroline Hoffman. To Mason, Caroline "seemed to have something of the strength of a goddess," and he compares the rustle of her dress when she walks to "the sound of Diana on the forest leaves" (1:345). Like a troubadour of old, Mason worships Caroline from afar, suffering "everything rather than reveal his emotions," but waiting for a moment of strength in which he can "open his heart." Unfortunately, the slightest intimate contact with Caroline leaves him desperately weak: he collapses one evening after tremulously buttoning her glove and suffers a dangerous relapse after they have taken a carriage ride. Caroline's discreet solicitude both tempts and bewilders her cousin, but her feeling is little more than sisterly. Mason revels in the frustration of loving the unattainable, but his deepest desire is for a permanence beyond any that love can provide. Like many of James' earliest heroes, Mason ultimately desires, not a stable identity in life, but the absolute stability of death. He becomes consciously aware of his deepest longings, however, only after he learns that Caroline has become engaged to his attending physician. His death wish finds ritualistic fulfillment when, weak with illness and fortifying himself with draughts of wine, he follows Caroline to a party. Seeing her "shining like a queen and fronted by a semicircle of men" (1:363), he approaches and takes her hand in an act of homage. Upon returning home, he prepares his will and dies a few weeks later.

Actually, Mason has sought death from the very beginning of his love. Although he tells himself that he will declare his passion as a mature man when he recovers, he wills his relapses during moments of intimacy because they impose the barriers to sexual union upon which his self-flagellant imagination thrives. Agony becomes love's perverse delectation, and death becomes its final fulfillment when the love image is irrevocably beyond reach. Although Mason's case may have seemed "extraordinary" to the American readers of its day, it is a common one in James' early fiction. In "Poor Richard" (1867), a dissolute and unpromising youth declares his adoration for a reserved young heiress, who seems to him "a goddess . . . a creature unattainable." The lady offers only friendship, and, when Richard is convinced that she can never love him, he resumes his drinking and becomes dangerously ill with typhoid. In "Osborne's Revenge" (1868), the writer Robert Graham becomes infatuated with a modest young girl whom he meets at a resort. Envisioning her as a cruel, icy Diana, he complains to a friend that she has poisoned his life, grows progressively weaker, and finally commits suicide after she rejects him. In "A Passionate Pilgrim" (1871), an emotionally disturbed American traveler falls in love with his cousin, a rich English spinster. Searle wishes only to worship this gentle lady, and his health breaks down completely when her domineering brother forbids him to see her. Although the brother is eventually killed in a fall from his horse, Searle, like Mason, is really in love with death, and he peacefully expires when his cousin comes to visit him. In Searle's mind, the woman becomes an embodiment of death itself. "Let me today do a mad, sweet thing," he begs after their first meeting, "Let me fancy you the soul of all the dead women who have trod these terrace flags which lie here like sepulchral tablets in the pavement of a church. Let me say I worship you" (2:264).

Self-destruction, Rougemont has observed, is the underlying desire of all courtly lovers.[25] James' heroes, however, unlike Tristram, Shakespeare's Antony, Goethe's Eduard, or Brontë's Heathcliff, seek death, not as a means to numinous union with their beloved, but as oblivion, as an escape from consciousness altogether. In this respect, their passion resembles the despiritualized, masochistic love that Mario Praz traces through the nineteenth century in *The Romantic Agony*. James' "belle inhumaine," however, is a very different creature from the "belle dame sans merci" of Keats, Flaubert, Baudelaire, Gautier, and Swinburne. Although the worshipers of both types of women take pleasure in their pain and long for the finality of death, the lover of Venus is "the powerless victim of the furious rage of a beautiful woman,"[26] whereas the lover of Diana is the victim of his own self-destructive imagination. Swinburne's and Baudelaire's characters are drained by a vampire woman; James' characters drain themselves.

James' fascination with the destructive nature of love began long before his career as a writer. In *Notes of a Son and Brother*, he recalls reading Prosper Mérimée's strange story of a statue of Venus who becomes enamoured of a mortal man, comes to life, and crushes him to death in her embrace; the future novelist found himself "fluttering deliciously—quite as if with a sacred terror—at the touch of 'La Venus d'Ille.' "[27] The story struck his "immaturity as a masterpiece of art and offered to the young curiosity . . . the sharpest of all challenges for youth, the challenge as to the special source of the effect." When James turned thirty, he was still exploring the source of this peculiar "effect," and, in "The Last of the Valerii'' (1874), he recast Mérimée's tale in the light of his own psychological assumptions. Transforming Venus into a milder pagan deity, James reversed the love relationship and told the story of a man's perverse infatuation with a statue. In so doing, he shifted the destructive energy from the marble image to Count Valerio's imagination.

What is most significant about the tale, perhaps, is its location: the pitted, mouldering Italian landscape becomes an unmistakable metaphor for the dark profane impulses buried in the hero's psyche. Before the Count brings his New England wife, Martha, to his crumbling villa in Rome, he confesses to being ''a poor Catholic.'' His remark is a considerable understatement, for the narrator detects in him a strain that is decidedly anti-Christian, ''a dark efflorescence of the evil germs which history had implanted in his line'' (3:107). As the story develops, these evil germs give rise to a diseased love. While excavating the ruins of the villa one day, Valerio's workmen unearth the statue of an ancient goddess. Even the American narrator senses a mysterious beauty in the figure: ''She seemed to me colossal, though I afterwards perceived that she was of perfect human proportions. My pulses began to throb, for I felt she was something great, and it was great to be among the first to know her. Her marvelous beauty gave her an almost human look, and her absent eyes seemed to wander back at us'' (3:100). So forcibly is the Count struck with the statue's perfectly immobilized human loveliness that he begins to feel a human passion for her. Soon, this adoration usurps his love for his wife: he sets the goddess in a little temple where he keeps nightly vigils, prostrating himself before her in a delirium of ecstasy. Although the archeologist who uncovered the statue speculates that it is Valerii's Juno, she is not the matronly Juno worshiped by the Greeks, but one whose imperious purity seems more an attribute of Artemis. James emphasizes the statue's resemblance to the moon goddess in the tale's climactic scene, in which the narrator finds Valerio lying senseless at the foot of the altar. ''The casement yielded to my pressure, turned on its hinges, and showed me what I had been looking for—Juno visited by Diana. The beautiful image stood bathed in the radiant flood and shining with a purity which made her most persuasively divine" (3:114).

The moonlight that filters into the shrine bathes both the "belle inhumaine" and her ministrant in a ghostly pallor, marking "the shining image as a goddess indeed," and blanching Valerio's face, "which seemed already pale with weariness." James' imagery is significant here, for the Count's self-destructive longing transforms the virgin into a vampire in his imagination: the face of the statue seems to glow as her lover's becomes pale.[28] The meaning of this analogy becomes clearer when the narrator discovers blood on the altar face. Suppressing a "swarm of hideous conjectures," he suggests that this "curious glitter" was produced by a sacrificial lamb or calf. The explanation seems dubious, given the degree of Valerio's obsession, and James rather daringly insinuates that Valerio has inflicted a self-emasculating wound. Ritual castration would be a fitting prelude to death for the heroes of James' early tales, both because it heightens the pain-pleasure of self-abasement, and because it insures that the love-image will be sexually unattainable. In Valerio's case, self-mutilation would also be an appropriate expression of his buried pagan heritage: Frazer notes that Diana demanded chastity of her followers and, on at least one occasion, used bloodshed to punish impurity. In pagan ceremonies for the goddess Cybele, young men would castrate themselves in glorification of the deity. Next to suicide, the castration ritual suggests man's strongest longing for stasis; just as the virgin seems a fixed image by virtue of her inviolable purity, her worshiper seeks permanence by symbolically denying his capacity for sexual change. Unlike Graham, Mason, and Searle, Count Valerio is finally unable to fulfill his love through self-destruction. At the end of the tale, he is persuaded to bury his love-image in the ground from which it came. This gesture, however, does not imply a solution to the Count's obsession, for its psychological equivalent is merely the repression of his suicidal impulse.

Like Valerio's death wish, James' deep-seated fascination with the mind's capacity to prey upon itself did not end at the conclusion of the tale. Four years after "The Last of the Valerii," it surfaced again in one of the most unpleasant tales he would ever write, "Longstaff's Marriage." Reginald Longstaff, already in poor health, meets wealthy Diana Belfield, a "fiercely virginal" young woman with a "tall light figure . . . nobly poised head . . . and a rapid gliding step" (4:209). Typically, James' hero imagines her as "a beautiful statue," a "goddess treading the forest leaves." Like his predecessors, Longstaff yearns to die, and the worship of a beautiful virgin provides him with both a romantic justification and a dramatic framework in which to fulfill his desire. While Diana receives with indifference the attention of a flock of suitors, Longstaff wastes away, adoring her from afar. One day, when he feels his end near at hand, he summons the courage to tell the girl's friend Agatha of his love. To heighten the anguish of his demise, he then sends a message to Diana, asking her to marry him on his death bed and so inherit his fortune. Diana refuses, observing, "If he could die with it [her consent], he could die without it" (4:230). At this point, a peculiar phenomenon occurs—Longstaff falls out of love and is restored to health. He later explains that injured pride impelled his recovery, but it is more probable that death lost its appeal when Diana denied him the ultimate frustration—that of marrying a beautiful virgin and dying on the brink of possessing her.

Two years later, Longstaff meets Diana in Rome and is astonished to find her languid and sickly. This time it is Diana who is dying—dying of love for him! Like Longstaff, she had longed for death from the beginning and refused any marriage that might rekindle life in her. Her love for Longstaff crystallized when she saw him on the verge of extinction: whereas he had seen her as a means to death, Diana saw in the stricken man an incarnation of death itself. Her love and illness began at the exact moment Longstaff's ended. At the end of the tale, James' hero grants the wish that Diana had denied him by accepting her proposal of marriage; his bride then achieves the end that she had earlier denied him by her refusal—she dies. Although the painfully symmetrical structure of the story hints at a psychological symbiosis between the lovers, each is entirely trapped within the realm of his own mind.

CHAPTER TWO

As James reveals over and over again in these tales, it is the private consciousness that brings about its own extinction just as it creates the images it adores.

It is difficult to read many of the tales that James composed during the first decade of his career without asking oneself why a writer so conscious of the perils of image-love should be so obsessed with it in his fiction. In most of these stories, the author's attitude toward his hero seems a curious mixture of sympathetic identification and ironic detachment. In works such as "The Passionate Pilgrim," "The Last of the Valerii," and "The Madonna of the Future," James creates this tone by telling the lover's story from the point of view of an observing friend, who is both deeply concerned about the protagonist's welfare and acutely aware of his delusion. In others, like "Osborne's Revenge" and "The Story of a Masterpiece," he establishes a double focus by dividing the love story between two men—one rational, one blindly romantic—who fall in love with the same woman.

These early narrative devices were, in part, outgrowths of an aesthetic tenet that James had set down in 1865: "A story based upon those elemental passions in which we seek the true and final manifestation of character must be told in a spirit of intellectual superiority to those passions."[29] As Leon Edel points out, however, James' attitude toward his characters reveals an ambivalence deep within the writer himself. Clearly, the insecure, hyperimaginative, self-defeating heroes of the early tales represent a part of James—the oppressed and romantically frustrated young man who felt overshadowed by his father and brother and doomed to aloof, passive observation in a turbulent world, who loved his cousin from across an unbridgeable divide, and who found himself trembling with "a sacred terror" at the thought of feminine destructiveness. Just as clearly, however, James recognized these dangerous traits in himself and learned to control them by distilling them in characters like Poor Richard, Ferdinand Mason, and Clement Searle. His early stories were not simply investigations into the psychopathology of love, but exorcisms. Although the

formal craftsman in James would have rebelled at D. H. Lawrence's observation that novelists "shed their sicknesses" in their
fiction, he recognized the purgative power of literary creation.
Even as a twenty-one-year-old novice, he understood that the
labor of writing a story somehow purified his life. "My *work* is my
salvation," he wrote in 1864,

> If this great army of puppets came forth at my simple bid-
> ding, then indeed I should die of their senseless clamor. But
> as the matter stands, they are my very good friends. The
> pains of labor regulate and consecrate my progeny. If it were
> as easy to write novels as to read them, then, too, my
> stomach might rebel against the phantom peopled atmosphere
> which I have given myself to breathe.[30]

In his first major novel, *Roderick Hudson*, James most fully
dramatized the conflicting traits in his own temperament—romantic and rational, artistic and analytic, self-defeating and self-
sustaining. Edel suggests that, in creating the passionate young
sculptor, Roderick, and his reserved benefactor, Rowland, the
novelist "abstracted the incandescence of his genius and placed it
beside his decorous, cautious, restrained self."[31] In so doing,
James revealed the limitations of two opposing orientations toward
experience—particularly toward the experiences of art and love.
Both protagonists are intensely committed to sculpture, but each
feels trapped within himself and longs to give shape to his life
through the love of a woman. At this point, all similarities end.

Although Roderick seems to live from moment to moment "in a
single sustained pulsation," he is actually devoted to an image of
eternal beauty, both as an artist and as a lover. Indeed, his aesthetic and romantic senses are so interdependent that, like Theobald, he comes to believe that his artistic ideal exists in flesh and
blood. After a fleeting glimpse of Christina Light, he falls five
fathoms deep in love and immediately declares that he must preserve her image in marble. "She's beauty itself," he tells Rowland, "She's a revelation. I don't believe she is living—she's a
phantasm, a vapour, an illusion."[32] Roderick momentarily doubts

the reality of the girl's physical appearance, but this outer beauty, unlike Serafina's, is genuine—only Roderick's conception of her inner purity is illusory. Shortly after their first meeting, he pictures Christina shining down with a divine light upon the little boys of a Jesuit school. Rather than looking up at Christ, the imagined children gaze at Christina. The irony of Roderick's fantasy is implicit in Christina's name: her "light" is not an inner spiritual glow that radiates outward, but a surface glimmer cast upon her by the adoring eyes of the male world. We find in this girl with the "dusky locks" the seeds of such Jamesian dark women as Madame Merle, Kate Croy, and Charlotte Stant—women who conceive of themselves primarily in terms of their manners, habits, and tastes, and who strive to create a visible image of themselves for others to admire.

Christina is psychologically akin to Roderick (and distinct from Rowland and Mary Garland) in her desire to define herself in relation to some fixed external; her deepest longing is "to get out of myself" (p. 138), and she dreams of an ideal man, "a strong, positive, imperious person," who will help her to do so. The crucial difference is that she realizes her ideal to be merely a dream and feels condemned always to inhabit the realm of her own ego. Incapable of believing in anything outside herself, Christina finds that she is also incapable of loving anyone beyond herself. The only behavior that relieves her sense of self-entrapment consists of projecting her fantasies outward, performing on a social stage the roles that she imagines. Whereas Roderick is a sculptor in love, chiseling out a single figure in his imagination, Christina is an actress who plays at passion, a kind of female Oscar Wilde, "fond of histrionics for their own sweet sake." Rowland quickly realizes that "she had a fictitious history in which she believed much more fondly than in her real one, and an infinite capacity for extemporised reminiscence adapted to the mood of the hour. She liked to idealize herself, to take interesting and picturesque attitudes to her own imagination . . ." (p. 184). Before the eyes of the world, she is both saint and seductress, "half a ballerina and half a madonna," a little girl with an outlandish poodle and a goddess in a vaporous white gown. But, to Roderick's eyes, she remains the image that he carved in marble. This adoration of Christina gradually drains him of all other inspiration; by focusing his imaginative energy upon a fixed ideal, the artist alienates himself from the ocean of sensations and impressions that once inspired him. Christina's inescapable marriage to the Prince Casamassima finally shatters Roderick's image and drives him to an apparently suicidal fall from a cliff. Shortly before his death, he describes the sense of disembodied isolation that haunts so many of James' characters: "Look at this lovely world and think what it must be to be dead to it! . . . Dead, dead; dead and buried! Buried in an open grave, where you lie staring up at the sailing clouds, smelling the waving flowers and hearing all nature live and grow above you! That's the way I feel" (p. 306).

By 1875, James seemed convinced that this drifting world of private impressions was the only reality that man could ever know. He realized, too, that, although we need not passively yield to its changes, we have to accept them to go on living. Each individual was enclosed within the dome of his own awareness, but to love an image was simply to interpose another pane of glass between consciousness and the world outside. In "Rose-Agatha," a tale of 1878, James parodies all the imaginative lovers of his earlier fiction in Sanguinetti. When this effeminate collector of bric-a-brac tells the narrator that he has fallen hopelessly in love with a nameless beauty whom he saw in a beauty salon window, his friend assumes that he is infatuated with the proprietress. Sanguinetti's love is actually a wax dummy, and, by the end of the tale, he has removed the bust to his apartment, grotesquely mounted her on a pedestal, and dressed her in a full-length gown. This satirical little tale would be trivial beyond mention if it did not reflect an attitude toward private experience that James expressed most clearly in an essay written just before *Roderick Hudson*. Using the timeworn metaphor of life as battle, he asserts the grim necessity of living with a consciousness of flux.

Life *is*, in fact, a battle. Evil is insolent and strong; beauty enchanting but rare; goodness very apt to be weak; folly very apt to be defiant; wickedness to carry the day; imbeciles to be in great places, people of sense in small, and mankind, generally, unhappy. But the world as it stands is no illusion, no phantasm, no evil dream of a night; we wake up to it again for ever and ever; we can neither forget it, nor deny it, nor dispense with it. We can welcome experience as it comes, and give it what it demands, in exchange for something which it is idle to pause to call much or little so long as it contributes to swell the volume of consciousness. In this there is mingled pain and delight, but over the mysterious mixture there hovers a visible rule, that bids us learn to will and seek to understand.[33]

The chaos of experience is inevitable, James suggests, and we can only choose to be dead or alive to it. Living, however, demands more than merely submitting to experience; it entails searching for sources of inner order even as we recognize our continual transformations. James insists that, amid the intensities of pain and delight, we exercise our vital will and seek self-understanding.

Clearly, if love was ever to liberate man from the chaos of his own psyche and place him in some self-defining relation to another, it would have to go beyond the images created by the conscious mind and tap a deeper wellspring of life. Above all, lovers would have to recognize the continual transformations taking place within themselves, their beloved, and the world at large. Twenty-five years after *Roderick Hudson*, James would suggest a new source of identity in a love that arose from the individual unconscious, but, during the intervening years, his characters struggle ineffectually to realize a self-defining love while remaining aware, to varying degrees, of phenomenological change. Rowland Mallet is the first of James' heroes to perceive his beloved as something other than a timeless icon. Whereas Roderick, the sculptor, falls in love with a face and form, Rowland, the cautious critic, seeks an elusive spiritual beauty that emerges gradually with the deepening understanding of another's personality. Upon meeting Roderick's American fiancée, he notes that "Mary Garland had not the countenance to inspire a sculptor"; yet "when you had made this observation, you had somehow failed to set it down against her, for you had already passed from measuring contours to tracing meanings. In Mary Garland's face there were many possible ones, and they might give you the more to think about . . ." (p. 39). Rowland realizes that the girl's beauty is visible only to those who see with an inward eye, those willing to look beneath immediate appearances and to weigh subtle and often contradictory impressions.

Philip Rahv, Oscar Cargill, and others have compared Mary to Hawthorne's allegorical figures in *The Blithedale Romance* and *The Marble Faun*. This analogy is misleading, however, for, although Mary's New England innocence contrasts sharply with Christina's European "corruption," she possesses a capacity for inner change that is totally alien to Hawthorne's Priscilla and Hilda. Mary's character, like her face, is unfinished, and her sense of herself changes as she assimilates more and more new impressions. During her stay in Italy, this child of Puritanism can admit, "This place has destroyed any scrap of consistency that I ever possessed, but, even if I may say something sinful, I love it." Ostensibly, Mary seems perfectly suited for Rowland, who serves as her guide in Rome and encourages her to accept the pain of self-transformation. "One's in for it one way or another," he tells her, "and one might as well do it with a good grace as with a bad; since one can't escape life, it's better to take it by the hand" (p. 221). Unfortunately, Mary follows this advice too well: she is so intoxicated by her sip of Italy and so fascinated by the development of her own consciousness that she becomes psychologically self-sufficient. After Roderick's death, she is content to dwell alone with her impressions—even in an American village. Although Rowland, with infinite patience, is still courting her at the end of the novel, there seems little hope that she will ever return his love.

In *Roderick Hudson*, as in the three long novels that follow in the 1880s, James seems to inquire whether romantic love is possible at all without a belief in fixed ideals. If the images that we adore are illusions, so too, he implies, may be love itself. How can we love another person who is merely part of a swarm of quickly dissolving impressions in our own mind? As James developed his fiction, his unresolved doubts about the limits of human experience gave rise to two overwhelming questions, which he formulated most precisely in *The Portrait of a Lady*: is it possible to drink deeply from the cup of private experience and still remain capable of loving another? Is it possible to recognize the spontaneity of the self and still discover a source of psychological order?

Before James could maturely address these questions, much less answer them, he had to broaden the concept of experience in his work. During the late 1870s, he was becoming aware that, although each individual dwells within the theatre of his own impressions, he also exists as part of an ever-shifting social galaxy. For James, the private mind's impressions of the densely populated outer world constitute experience at the highest pitch of intensity. To be saturated in a world of varied tastes, customs, and values was to be most fully alive—and this is precisely what James and his protagonists find in Europe. In most of the fiction before *Roderick Hudson*, however, the novelist seems hardly aware of man's social relations at all; the central action of most of the early tales takes place entirely within the hero's mind, and in some, like "The Story of a Masterpiece" and "A Most Extraordinary Case," it seems to unfold outside time and space altogether. This phenomenon is partly explained by James' consuming interest in the psychological side of man, but, as he complained to William Dean Howells in early 1880, it was difficult to consider man in any interesting social context when one lived in a homogeneous American society. In a letter, he responded to Howells' assertion that an American writer could find sufficient inspiration in his native land:

I sympathize even less with your protest against the idea that it takes an old civilization to set a novelist in motion—a proposition that seems to me so true as to be a truism. It is on manners, customs, usages, habits, forms, upon all these things matured and established, that a novelist lives—they are the very stuff his work is made of; and in saying that in the absence of these "dreary and worn-out paraphernalia" which I enumerate as being wanting in our American society, "we have simply the whole of human life left," you beg (to my sense) the question. I should say we had just so much less of it as these same "paraphernalia" represent, and I think they represent an enormous quantity of it.[34]

Much of the sentiment that James expressed to Howells had informed his book-length study of Hawthorne the year before. There, the rising star of American letters had wondered aloud how his illustrious forefather had written novels at all, given all "the items of high civilization . . . which are absent from the texture of American life."[35] These missing ingredients, as James proceeds to enumerate them, range from an aristocracy and a sporting class to "thatched cottages" and "ivied ruins." Ironically, at the time of this critique, James himself had written only one novel that attempted to analyze European society, *The American* in 1877. Although *Roderick Hudson* and stories like "The Madonna of the Future" and "The Last of the Valerii" are set in Italy, the society and culture serve as little more than a backdrop for James' examination of the relationship between art, love, and madness. Apart from Count Valerii, who seems almost too fatuous to be real, the major characters of all these works are of American origin. In the mid-1870s, however, James came into contact with two groups of people who helped to modify his portrayal of love and its relation to identity for the next fifteen years.

Immediately upon completing *Roderick Hudson*, he journeyed to France, where he made the acquaintance of Turgenev, Flaubert, Zola, and Edmond de Goncourt. Each in his way was committed to the novel of social realism, and James found in Turgenev a model for his own literary aspirations. Like the author of the *Comedie Humaine*, Turgenev explored human passions from both a psychological and a social point of view. "With Turgenev, as with Balzac," James wrote in 1875, "the whole person springs into being at once; the character is never left shivering for its fleshly envelope, its face, its figure, its gestures, its tone, its costume, its name, its bundle of antecedents."[36] James realized that most of his early protagonists were "shivering" for want of just these social characteristics. The three major novels of his middle period—*The Portrait of a Lady*, *The Princess Casamassima*, and *The Tragic Muse*—reflect the novelist's growing interest in presenting the psychology of love within a social matrix, as Balzac had done in *Eugénie Grandet* and Turgenev in *Fathers and Sons*.

More importantly, however, James' novels of the 1880s bear the unmistakable stamp of his own experience in the European social world. He had been established in London for four years when he wrote to Howells of the vapidity of American life, and he had come to appreciate the "customs, usages and habits" of an old, rigidly stratified civilization. He thought of himself no longer as a visitor to the Old World, but as a permanent resident, and he immersed himself in society so deeply that in 1879 he could write, rather apologetically, to Grace Norton of "having dined out during the past winter 107 times."[37] It was little wonder that James wrote to his sister the same year that his dinners were falling "into a sort of shimmering muddle."[38] These perpetual gatherings satisfied the novelist's appetite for experience, by serving up a rich mixture of human types: politicians and poets, bishops and scientists, aging professors and wealthy young widows, glittering flirts and portly matrons. It was in this variegated company that the pulse of life seemed to throb most intensely; and it was here, James realized, that the individual who wished to establish his identity faced the greatest challenge. As he would state most clearly in *The Awkward Age*, society was the element of flux itself: one could feel exhilarated by the multiplicity of one's sensations, or isolated and exhausted by them. "If you dine out a good deal in London," he wrote to William in 1879, "you forget your dinners the next morning—or rather, if you walk home, as I always do, you forget it by the time you have turned the corner to the street. My impressions evaporate with the fumes of the champagne."[39]

The titles that James gave to the two novels that he wrote immediately after *Roderick Hudson*—*The American* and *The Europeans*—reflect his broadening concern with portraying man's relationship to his national culture. More importantly, they hint at another kind of identity that the heroes and heroines of his middle period will struggle to establish. Early characters like Theobald and Roderick had existed only in relation to a love object; they sought identity purely in a subjective sense, as an invigorating sameness and psychic continuity. Isabel Archer of *The Portrait of a Lady* and Hyacinth Robinson of *The Princess Casamassima* carry on the quest for this kind of self-definition, but, as active participants in the crowded, multilayered outer world, they also struggle to discover their social role. The psychologist Erik Erikson points out that, in real life, psychological and social identity are part of a single process in the development of an individual. "In discussing identity," Erikson writes,

> . . . we cannot separate personal growth and communal change, nor can we separate . . . the identity crisis in individual life and contemporary crises in historical development because the two help to define each other and are truly relative to each other. In fact, the whole interplay between the psychological and the social, the developmental and the historical, for which identity formation is of prototypal significance, could be conceptualized only as a kind of *psychosocial relativity*.[40]

The already infinitely complex problem of discovering both a psychological and a social self is compounded by the human need to make these selves consistent—to appear in the world's eyes just as we appear in our own. Erikson underscores the problem involved in this process—a problem that is crucial to both Isabel and Hyacinth—when he observes that "mere 'roles' played interchangeably, mere self-conscious 'appearances,' or mere strenuous

CHAPTER TWO

'postures' cannot possibly be the real thing, although they may be dominant aspects of what today is called the 'search for identity.' "[41] James would have concurred with this statement; his protagonists never simply adopt poses, in the fashion of Christina Light, but rather seek to discover their truest psychological and social self by discovering someone outside themselves. In short, they fall in love.

The protagonists of James' long middle-period novels, although more conscious of transience and mutability in themselves and the world of their perceptions, still devote themselves to idealized lovers. The essential difference between characters such as Isabel, Hyacinth, and Nick Dormer and the heroes of the early tales is that these more mature characters seek not merely a fixed psychological relation in their love ideal, but a social role in life. The beloved comes to represent a class, a culture, a code of manners, a set of tastes, a whole mode of living with which the lover longs to identify himself. We see this kind of love developing in Christopher Newman, who prizes Claire de Cintre as an embodiment of aristocratic French refinement, in Daisy Miller, who fancies Giovanelli "a fine Italian gentleman," in Winterbourne, who both loves and fears Daisy as an image of American girlhood, and we find its fullest and most complex expression in Isabel's vision of Gilbert Osmond in *The Portrait of a Lady*.

THREE

The Requirements of the Imagination: *The Portrait of a Lady* and *The Princess Casamassima*

*Experience, as I see it, is our apprehension and our measure of
what happens to us as social creatures.*
HENRY JAMES

HENRY JAMES' first great novel, *The Portrait of a Lady*, began as a luminous portrait in his imagination. There had lingered in the novelist's mind for several years "the character and aspect of a particular engaging young woman" in the act of "affronting her destiny."[1] Her grasping intelligence and "moral spontaneity" made her the finest flower of American girlhood, yet she was endangered by "her meager knowledge, her inflated ideals, her confidence at once innocent and dogmatic, [and] her temper at once exacting and indulgent."[2] James had refrained from portraying this figure in his fiction prior to 1880 because of his pious desire to give his treasure a perfect setting. As he notes in his 1907 preface to the novel, his portrait required for its background a social matrix that would set off the finely etched psychology of the heroine without calling too much attention to itself. The chief problem, he recalls, lay in balancing "character" and "plot"; that is, in balancing "the young woman's own consciousness . . . her relation to herself," with her "relations" to the human "satellites" around her.[3] The heroine was to be isolated, working out her destiny for herself, yet existing also at the center of a complex social web, a "puzzle" full of "numbered pieces." James goes on to explain that the solution was to make his protagonist's relations to others always "contributive" to her developing sense of herself.

His remarks upon the evolution of the novel's form are germane here because they illuminate one of his central thematic concerns. Isabel Archer confronts a problem akin to the one that James faced in creating her: she must reconcile the demands of her own psyche with those of the world around her. More specifically, she must define both "her relation to herself" and her relation to society and strive to make that outer self that the world sees congruent with an inner sense of personality. James enunciates the distinction between these two aspects of identity (psychological and social) in a crucial exchange between Isabel and Madame Merle shortly after their meeting at Gardencourt. "When you've lived as long as I," Madame Merle instructs her young friend, "you'll see that every human being has his shell and that you must take the shell into account."

> There's no such thing as an isolated man or woman; we're each of us made up of some cluster of appurtenances. What shall we call our "self"? Where does it begin? where does it end? It overflows into everything that belongs to us—and then it flows back again. I know a large part of myself is in the clothes I choose to wear. I've a great respect for *things*. One's self—for other people—is one's expression of one's self; one's house, one's furniture, one's garments, the books one reads, the company one keeps—these things are all expressive (1:287-288).

As a high priestess of refined tastes, Serena Merle may be said to convert Ruskin's observation, "Tell me what you like and I'll tell you what you are," into a principle of personality formation. Her identity is self-created, defined completely and irrevocably by the figure she cuts in the external world. She exists only as an expression of her accumulated talents and possessions and would seem to evaporate outside a social climate. Ralph aptly describes her as "the great round world itself" (1:362), and James tells us that she had become . . . "too ripe and too final. She was in a word, too perfectly the social animal that man and woman are supposed to have been intended to be" (1:274).

Isabel, on the other hand, bluntly refuses to acknowledge that external manifestations or social displays can begin to reveal her own spontaneous, rapidly metamorphosing self. Identity, insofar as Isabel can conceptualize it at all early in the novel, is a mystically elusive property of individual consciousness, an inner light that vanishes as quickly as a particle of radium. "I don't know whether I succeed in expressing myself," she answers Madame Merle, "but I know that nothing else expresses me. Nothing that belongs to me is any measure of me; everything's on the contrary, a limit, a barrier, and a perfectly arbitrary one. Certainly the clothes . . . I choose to wear, don't express me. . . . My clothes may express the dressmaker, but they don't express me. . . . To begin with it's not my choice that I wear them; they're imposed upon me by society" (1:288).

James' use of Isabel and Madame Merle to explore diametrically opposed conceptions of identity bears a superficial similarity to his depiction of Mary Garland and Christina Light, but these early prototypes had functioned mainly to illuminate the personalities of the male protagonists. In *The Portrait*, however, James placed his women at center stage and, more important, endowed them with a keen awareness of what they represent in the intellectual dialectic of the novel. Isabel's contempt for social conventions, in particular, springs from her sensitive realization that obedience to them will encrust a false, inflexible disguise upon her unique, fluid inner self. Like the disciples of Bergson (and Pater), she revels in the "élan vital" of her being and dreads everything in society that is mechanical, static, and stereotypic. Possessing "an immense curiosity about life" and "a delicate, desultory, flamelike spirit" (1:69), her "deepest enjoyment [is] to feel the continuity between the movements of her own soul and the agitations of the world" (1:45). Paradoxically, this desire for continual self-development carries with it a need for almost self-induced blindness to particular realities in the outside world. Perfect happiness, she tells Henrietta Stackpole, would be riding in "a swift carriage, of a dark night, rattling with four horses over roads that one can't see" (1:235). After Mrs. Touchett appears like a fairy godmother and whisks her off to England, Isabel discovers that only the cultural refinement and complex variety of European society can fully sustain her passion for knowledge and self-development. The challenge that she faces, then, is to sample delicately the intellectual riches of this world without becoming trapped as a social fixture within it.

Isabel speaks for most of James' heroines when she remarks, "I'm very fond of my liberty" (1:24), but she is the first of them to realize the dilemma that unrestricted freedom imposes upon the individual. While total freedom offers an infinite range of potential experiences, the moment one commits oneself to any particular life-style or, in love, to any single individual, one forfeits one's freedom. Thus, Isabel declares early in the novel, "I don't wish to touch the cup of experience. It's a poisoned drink! I only want to see for myself" (1:213). The problem is, of course, that "seeing," as Isabel uses the word, is not really living or, as Ralph terms it, "feeling." After a year of perpetual travel, Isabel herself acknowledges that she has been engaged, "not [in] the act of living, but [in] that of observing" (2:82). To live, in the Jamesian sense, one must choose certain experiences and reject others; it is through such choices that we project a *social* identity. Isabel, however, with her inflated American ideal of sincerity, refuses to accept any social identity that does not express her true spiritual being. She insists that "her life should always be in harmony with the most pleasing impression she should produce," that she "would be what she appeared, and she would appear what she was" (1:69). James' heroine fails in this quest, not because she lacks the consciousness of perpetual change within herself, but because she remains blind to the deceptive complexity of minds outside her own. Only after her marriage does she relinquish her sense of the immutability of other personalities and cease to think of the European world as being "just like a novel" (1:18).

Although Isabel would chastise those who judge her by appearances, she forms her opinions of others on just such a superficial basis. She conceives of individuals as types and so rejects two suitors who, she imagines, would impose a false social identity upon her. The first of these is Lord Warburton, an amiable, impeccably mannered English aristocrat with a seat in Parliament, "a hundred thousand a year . . . and half a dozen houses to live in"

(1:102). Although Warburton is the product of a civilization infinitely more complex and subtly diversified than Isabel's own, she views him simply as the embodiment of a social class and fears that marriage to such a man would fix narrow limits upon her everexpanding consciousness. Although she is "lost in admiration of her opportunity" at his proposal, "she [manages] to move back into the deepest shade of it, even as some wild, caught creature in a vast cage" (1:153).

Isabel's indefatigable American suitor, Caspar Goodwood, makes his first appearance at Gardencourt on the heels of Warburton's failure. A man of resolute will and practical, if rather unimaginative, intelligence, he has inherited a cotton industry in Boston and become a kind of nineteenth-century tycoon, in the fashion of Christopher Newman. Unlike this American forerunner, however, Goodwood is completely impervious to the cultural seductions of Europe and remains rigidly mercantile, Puritan, and democratic to the end. Isabel senses something quintessentially masculine, yet frightening and inflexible, in his "supremely strong, clean make" (1:165); she thinks of him with discomfort as "a figure too straight and stiff," "a tireless watcher at a window," a "stubborn fact" (1:162). Like Warburton, he exists in her eyes more as an image than a man: "she saw the different fitted parts of him as she had seen, in museums and portraits, the different fitted parts of armoured warriors—in plates of steel handsomely inlaid with gold" (1:165). All the restrictive qualities that Isabel associates with industrialized America—its mechanical strength, its ostentatious wealth, its insensitivity to man's spiritual needs, its lack of cultural variety—coalesce in this vision. Goodwood, like Warburton, seems to her a creature of hard outward forms, and she senses in him "a want of easy consonance with the deeper rhythms of life" to which her own finely tuned consciousness pulsates (1:165). The young industrialist exerts a kind of raw sexual magnetism, but Isabel believes that to marry him would be to submit her fluid inner self to a prison of mechanical American conventions.

After Goodwood's departure and the death of Mr. Touchett,

however, James' heroine gradually begins to adopt a new attitude toward herself and her experience. Whereas she had previously rebelled at anything that threatened to inhibit her wide-ranging quest for new impressions, she comes to feel the need for some underlying principle of order in her personality. After her travels with Madame Merle, James tells us that "the desire for unlimited expansion had been succeeded in her soul by the sense that life was vacant without some private duty that might gather one's energies to a point" (2:82). This "more primitive need" for "private duty" demands, of course, that she select a particular way of life, and this, in turn, requires that she express some public version of herself. Although Isabel insists that her public and private selves correspond, she does not, like James' early heroes, wish to deny inner change altogether. She seeks, not a fixed image of herself, but rather a role that will, at once, express that which is truest and most permanent within her by narrowing the range of her experience and which will continue to promote her intellectual growth by refining that experience. The distinction between these two conceptions of integrated selfhood is crucial to the development of the identity theme in James' fiction: unlike self-images, which demand a belief in absolute stasis, roles require only a developing consistency of behavior, a deepening awareness of one's true, distinguishing characteristics. Further, while a self-image is merely an individual's idealized mental picture of himself, a role implies an awareness not only of one's interior personality, but of one's relation to an evaluating audience. The kind of self-definition that Isabel seeks is what Erik Erikson defines as "ego-identity," that is, "the awareness of the fact that there is [in the ego] a self-sameness and continuity . . . *the style of one's individuality*, and that this style coincides with the sameness and continuity of one's *meaning for significant others* in the immediate community."[4]

The driving force behind Isabel's need to establish her identity begins when her cousin Ralph persuades his dying father to leave her the lion's share of his inheritance—some 60,000 pounds. Ralph explains that his reason for wishing to make Isabel rich is to free her "to meet the requirements of her imagination" (1:261).

He believes that the money will "put wind in her sails," and he fancies her "going before the breeze" (1:260-262). Actually, Ralph hopes that Isabel will fulfill the requirements of his own imagination by living the kind of vital, freewheeling life that illness has denied him. His fondest desire is to see what life will make of her: to witness the rapid development of her intellect, to measure her responses to a myriad of people, places, and events, to watch her tastes broaden and her personality expand in a whirlpool of social activity. Ironically, the fortune through which he intends to liberate Isabel from all self-limiting choices has just the opposite effect. The money becomes the distinguishing fact about her and thus imposes upon her the burden of a widely recognized social stereotype—she finds that, in the world's eyes, she has become an heiress. "Now that you're a young woman of fortune," her aunt advises her, "you must know how to play the part—I mean play it well" (1:301). According to Mrs. Touchett, this requires that Isabel not only surround herself with "everything handsome," but also that she learn "to take care of" these supposed external manifestations of character. The great hazard of wealth, as James demonstrates in so much of his mature fiction, is that it leads others to view those who possess it simply in relation to their fortune. Like Milly Theale and Maggie Verver, Isabel finds herself a poor little rich girl condemned to live in a society that measures her weight only in gold. For Isabel, who resists social conventions and classifications more than any of James' other heroines, the stigma of affluence is especially false and uncomfortable. By the time she leaves for Italy with Mrs. Touchett, she feels an acute need to transfer the burden of her wealth to someone else's shoulders and to discover a truer role in life. Only gradually does it dawn upon her that she might fulfill both these desires in marriage—marriage, that is, to a particular kind of man.

Although Isabel's vision of life is unquestionably romantic, her fantasies of love are not romantic in the same way that Madame de Mauves', Daisy Miller's, or Catherine Sloper's are. Daisy, one suspects, would have found a more than adequate incarnation of her dream of love in Lord Warburton, and Catherine would have probably turned Goodwood into "a knight on horseback." Isabel's naiveté is far more complex. Although she admits that she "began to dream very young," she denies that she ever dreamed of "a young man with a fine moustache going down on his knees" to her (1:286). Beginning with Isabel, James' lovers transcend such conventional fantasies. They fall in love with images, to be sure, but with unique images that they create to fulfill their individual needs. Isabel's peculiar attitudes and circumstances make "the requirements of her imagination" in love extremely restrictive: her husband must free her from the false social role that her wealth enforces and provide her with one which, while true to her deepest instincts and sympathies, will not completely rigidify her elusive inner being. These requirements distinctively shape the contours of her romantic ideal: in order to be deserving of her fortune, her lover must be poor, in order to help her cultivate her truest self, he must be mature, sympathetic, and culturally refined, and, above all, in order to allow her to bring her psychological and social identities into correspondence, he must represent nothing conventional in the eyes of the world.

Isabel proceeds to fall in love with Gilbert Osmond, or, more correctly, with the image of a poor, solitary widower who has renounced all social intercourse and fled "the vulgar troubles" of the world to think "about art, beauty, and history" (1:377). Before she even meets Osmond, she has become infatuated with a shrewdly deceptive description of him that Madame Merle had planted in her mind months before: "The worst case [of indolence], I think, is a friend of mine, a countryman of ours. . . . He's Gilbert Osmond—he lives in Italy; that's all you can say about him or make of him. He's exceedingly clever, a man made to be distinguished; but, as I tell you, you exhaust the description when you say he's Mr. Osmond who lives *tout bêtement* in Italy" (1:281). So strong is Isabel's need to believe in this initial impression that she later views Osmond's gloomy Florentine villa, not as a soul's dungeon, but as a bastion in which her free spirit might comfortably and unrestrainedly reside. Mistaking mercenary greed for aesthetic refinement and vanity for taste, she concludes that Osmond "resembled no one she had ever seen; most people whom she knew might be divided into groups of a half a dozen specimens . . . he was a specimen apart" (1:375-376).

She carried away an image from her visit to his hill-top which her subsequent knowledge of him did nothing to efface and which put on for her a particular harmony with other supposed and divined things, histories within histories: the image of a quiet, clever, sensitive, distinguished man, strolling on a moss-grown terrace above the sweet Val d'Arno and holding by the hand a little girl (1:399).

This view of Osmond inspires in Isabel a correlative vision of herself, defines for her the role of a self-sacrificing wife and mother, quietly advancing, under her husband's guidance, in the cultivation of wisdom and beauty. It is through sympathy, generosity, and intellectual development that Isabel believes she will produce, both for society and herself, "her most pleasing impression." She is the first of James' characters to recognize that the greatest security in life lies in living, not for oneself, but for another. To share vicariously in another's commitment to experience is to gain a sense of inner cohesion by gathering all one's "energies" around that individual, while maintaining one's own precious reserve of freedom. Isabel therefore wishes to be, above all, selfless in her marriage, to serve Osmond and his daughter Pansy while living through them. Ralph stands in a similar relation to Isabel, but there is one essential difference. Whereas Ralph understands the mercurial nature of his cousin's personality and longs to see her change and grow with experience, Isabel frames Osmond as an unchanging portrait in her imagination. This fatal distortion of reality is born of a need so extraordinary that it promotes an almost willful self-deception. Prior to meeting her future husband, Isabel had "often reminded herself that there were essential reasons why one's ideal [of another person] could never become concrete. It was a thing to believe in, not to see—a matter of faith, not of experience" (1:266). No sooner does she hear about Osmond, however, than, James informs us that, for all her native intelligence and love of knowledge, "she had a natural shrinking from raising curtains and looking into dark corners" (1:284). Isabel's "fine capacity for ignorance" is really her reluctance to examine all of life with the full power of her consciousness, and this fear eventually causes her to misunderstand both Osmond and herself. Having determined to view her fiancé as a noble victim of society's injustice and misunderstanding, she regards the attacks upon him by Ralph, Mrs. Touchett, and Countess Gemini as virtual confirmations of his worthiness.

When James draws the curtain back three years after her marriage, we realize unmistakably that Osmond's fine aestheticism, generosity, and desire for privacy have been a sham and a delusion. In place of her ideal, Isabel finds a vain and vicious brute, an all-absorbing male ego who wishes to make his wife, along with his possessions, an extension of himself. "Her mind was to be his," she realizes, "attached to his own like a small garden-plot to a deer-park. . . . It would be a pretty piece of property for a proprietor already far-reaching" (2:200). Like Desdemona, Isabel fell in love with the imagined sufferings her husband had borne, but she finds herself married, not to Othello, but to Iago. Beneath Osmond's good manners, cleverness, and amenity, "his egotism lay hidden like a serpent in a bank of flowers" (2:196). Isabel comes to realize that her husband's egotism (like all egotism) can be gratified only by an admiring audience, and that this admiration can be won only through a complete submission to the values, standards, and customs of society. Far more than Warburton, or Goodwood, more even than Madame Merle, Osmond defines himself in relation to worldly proprieties. Dorothea Krook acutely describes his brand of hypocrisy as a "sophisticated conventionality . . . which is not the less but the more shabby and shoddy for being sophisticated, which affects to despise the world, but in fact submits itself and conforms itself wholly to the standards of the world. . . ."[5] As Krook also observes, however, Osmond is no less deceived by his ideal of Isabel than she is by her ideal of him. He has made Isabel conform to his demands partly by force of will; but he had envisioned her as a richly receptive and willing adjunct to his personality, a social ornament, a finely embellished mirror reflecting his own tastes, opinions and ambitions. Although husband and wife may suffer under similar delusions, the psychological needs that underlie their errors are poles apart. Whereas Isabel fell in love with an ideal of otherness and longed to define her role *in relation to* her beloved, Osmond, who is capable only of self-love, sought to enlarge his identity by making an ideal of feminine beauty an expression of himself. As a living portrait in his gallery, Isabel finds herself framed by social forms and displayed each night before the vulgar and acquisitive, the blandishing and the backbiting. In her role of perpetual hostess, she is condemned to wear a mask that bears no resemblance to the inner self that she had imagined.

It would be wrong, however, to view Isabel simply as a victim of Osmond's selfishness, for, in acquiescing to the conventions of her marriage, she is also victimized by her own indestructible pride. Ever determined to think well of herself, she insists upon bearing the burden of her unhappiness alone. She realizes with horror that to disobey her husband, to let the mask slip before others, would be an open "admission that their whole attempt" at marriage "had proved a failure." For all their moral differences, Isabel and Osmond share this intense fear of social failure, a similarity that gives rise to a perverse covenant between them. Only a few years after their wedding, Isabel finds herself bound to Osmond, not by the sanctity of their marriage vows, but by an unspoken agreement to deceive society, to perpetuate the illusion of contentment by "living together decently" in their established roles. Osmond's egotism would never allow him to break such a bond, and, even after Isabel has defied him by going to England and confessing her misery to the dying Ralph, she feels its moral force drawing her back to Rome, drawing her back, as her husband imagines it, to "the observation of a magnificent form" (2:336).

The identity conflict that James dramatizes at the end of *The Portrait of a Lady*—that which arises from the split between a psychologically idealized self and an enforced social role—becomes more and more acute for the protagonists of his middle-period novels. Already cut off from genuine contact with others by the barrier of subjective awareness, these characters are also separated from their ideal of true personality by a false public mask. Like Isabel, they each seek a perfect lover who, by helping them to live up to their true role, will allow them to integrate the public and private halves of their identity. Verena Tarrant of *The Bostonians* (1886) finds herself trapped in the public spotlight as a feminist orator after she has come to believe that "her real self" lies in marriage to Basil Ransom.[6] Gaston Probert of *The Reverberator* (1888), who "wanted to be as American as he could and yet not less French than he was," is torn between his social image as a Parisian aristocrat and his belief that he will fulfill his truest calling as the husband of an obscure American girl.[7] Nick Dormer and Peter Sherringham of *The Tragic Muse* (1890) both struggle to reconcile their political roles with their deeper aesthetic aspirations: Nick is a member of Parliament who longs to be a painter, Peter, a diplomat who feels most himself at the theatre. Both fall in love with Miriam Rooth, a young actress and model who evokes their deepest sense of artistic identity.

More than any other character from this period, Hyacinth Robinson of *The Princess Casamassima* (1886) embodies James' vision of bifurcated personality, of a sensitive human being caught in a false social role. Like Isabel, Hyacinth arrives at this condition only after he has spent most of the novel questing for his true self. The central ideological dispute in the novel between art and social action, between a beautiful but degenerate past and a pure but vapid future, finds expression in the young bookbinder's "mixed divided nature."[8] His confusion of identity is a direct outgrowth of the conditions of his birth. Raised by his adoring foster mother Pinnie in the depths of a London tenement, he has been encouraged to believe that he is actually the son of an aristocrat. Hyacinth's real heritage, as he later discovers, is radically mixed: he is the illegitimate son of a poor French adventuress and a British lord whom she stabbed to death. Having made this discovery in his adolescence, he finds that "there was no peace for him between the two currents that flowed in his nature" (2:264). He feels "that it might well be his fate to be divided to the point of torture, to be split open by sympathies that pulled him in different ways" (1:171). As he begins to speculate about the dim, confused legend of his mother's history, he finds that his imagination "supplied him, first and last, with a hundred different theories of his identity" (1:172).

> He didn't really know if he were French or were English, or which of the two he should prefer to be. His mother's blood, her suffering in an alien land, the unspeakable, unremediable misery that consumed her in a place and among a people she must have execrated—all this made him French; yet he was conscious at the same time of qualities that didn't mix with it (1:112).

While Hyacinth feels that he is a man without a country, he is even more intensely aware that he is a man without a class. As a plebeian, who "sprang up . . . out of the London pavement,"[9] he is filled with a passionate love for the downtrodden; but it is a love that struggles against his ever-deepening sense that he is composed of finer clay than his neighbors, that he is meant for a different kind of life.

The diffuse, seething world of lower-class London seems to offer Hyacinth no discernible role at all. He is morbidly aware of his own insignificance and realizes that his own circle "was an infinitesimally small shallow eddy in the roaring vortex of London." Beyond this chaos, Hyacinth sees the shimmering vision of an alter ego, an identity formed and stabilized by the timeless form and stability of the British aristocracy. As he grows up, "his imagination plunge[s] again and again into the flood that whirled past it and round it, in the hope of being carried to some brighter, happier vision—the vision of societies where, in splendid rooms, with smiles and soft voices, distinguished men, with women who were both proud and gentle, talked of art, literature and history" (1:140-141).

Hyacinth belongs to a long line of Jamesian heroes and heroines who cherish, above all, an ideal of personal sincerity. He wishes "to go through life in his own character," but, in his uncertainty as to what this character consists of, he feels "foredoomed" to wear "a mask . . . a borrowed mantle . . . to be every day and every hour an actor" (1:86). Like Isabel, Hyacinth longs for a role that will come naturally, one that will express his deepest traits and instincts and integrate some private ideal of self with a social image. Isabel had eschewed identification with any particular social class or political ideology (rejecting the aristocratic in Warburton and the democratic in Goodwood), but Hyacinth, because his crisis of identity is rooted in class confusion, seeks to define himself within these spheres. Thus, guided by his conflicting sympathies, he is drawn toward both the aristocracy and the anarchist revolution.[10] This revolution, although it occasionally uses the rhetoric of socialism, is committed, not to rebuilding society upon egalitarian ideals, but merely to its destruction. Its chief vehicle for social action is personal terrorism—the kind of personal terrorism to which Hyacinth fatally commits himself. As a young man in search of his identity, Hyacinth's attraction to the anarchist movement may seem peculiar, since anarchy is ideologically incompatible with the kind of social identity that he seeks—an identity based upon a recognition of definite class distinctions. What attracts Hyacinth most deeply in the movement, however, are not its anarchist aims, which he does not really understand until late in the novel, but, rather, the group identity, the sense of a personal role that it provides.

In his preface to the New York edition of the novel, James speaks of his hero "watching the same public show, the same innumerable appearances, I had watched myself, and . . . watching very much as I had watched."[11] As the statement suggests, the novelist distilled in his hero his own capacity for social observation, and the most distinctively Jamesian trait that Hyacinth inherited is his habit of viewing life in terms of dramatic scenes. There are two social stages upon which Hyacinth seeks to play a role: the circle of revolutionists that gathers at the Sun and Moon, headed by Paul Muniment, and the elegant aristocratic world that he sees embodied by the Princess Casamassima. These groups represent not simply antithetical class values, but Hyacinth's two conflicting ideals of himself. Sitting among his fellow revolutionaries, he "waited for the voice that should allot him the particular part he was to play. His ambition was to play it with brilliancy, to offer an example—an example even that might survive him—of pure youthful, almost juvenile, consecration" (1:343). Later, after his part has theoretically been assigned, he speaks of the assassination plot as "a great rehearsal" (2:49). At the same time, Hyacinth thinks of his hours with the Princess as a series of scenes from "a romance bound in vellum and gold." During their first meeting in the theatre box, he feels that being "enthroned with fine ladies in a dusky, spacious receptacle which framed the bright picture of the stage . . . made one's own situation seem a play within the play" (1:208). When he visits her at Medley soon afterward, he fears that to make a wrong movement of any sort would "cause the curtain to fall" (1:286). On "the stage of his inner consciousness," Hyacinth alternately sees himself as a daring revolutionary with a smoking pistol and as mannered gentleman surrounded by pretty women, richly bound books, and rare paintings.

The young man's belief in these incompatible roles is entirely dependent upon his love for Paul Muniment and the Princess, who represent to his imagination the highest, most incorruptible values of their respective worlds. Hyacinth seeks to define himself within each of these worlds by gaining the love of an ideal representative. He hopes to establish his true role in life in relation to someone whose social identity had been immutably confirmed. Hyacinth's love for Paul, which grows out of his "dream of friendship," is actually a one-sided adoration. Small, obscure, and confused, he stands in relation to the tall, forthright chemist much as a young boy does to an idealized older brother; he adopts his political attitudes and values out of a fervent desire to become like him. In his enthusiasm, Hyacinth fails to realize not only that Muniment feels indifference toward him, but that his ultimate goal as an insurgent is not social reform but personal power. It is through his misguided devotion to Paul, not to the anarchist movement, that

Hyacinth agrees to sacrifice his life for the revolution. And it is this ideal of friendship that inspires his hopelessly paradoxical desire for precise social definition in a group dedicated to the elimination of all social distinctions.

Hyacinth's countervailing love for the Princess, though born of an even greater self-deception than his affection for Paul, is purely romantic. He is "dazzled" from the moment he meets her at the theatre and comes to think of her as "something antique and celebrated, something that he had admired of old—in a statue, in a picture, in a museum" (1:207). Just as the Princess herself seems a work of art, so too she represents for Hyacinth the class that has produced and exhibited most of the art of our civilization. During his visit to her country estate, "his sensibility swung back from the objects that sprang up by the way, every one of which was a rich image of something he longed for, to the most beautiful woman in England, who sat there, well before him, as completely for his benefit as if he had been a painter engaged to paint her portrait" (2:28). As James demonstrates so frequently in his fiction, the belief in personal identity demands a sense of fixed relationship with another individual, so that conceptions of the self hinge upon delusive images of others. The sad irony of Hyacinth's adoring love is that, while it crystallizes his vision of himself as an aristocrat, it alienates the Princess, who is interested in him only as a working class revolutionary. When she discovers that he is only a halfhearted anarchist, she discards him. It is a mark of Hyacinth's desperate need to believe in his own aristocratic character that he is able to love the Princess as a permanent embodiment of the very class she repudiates. Although he hears her swear "by Darwin and Spencer and all the scientific iconoclasts as well as by the revolutionary spirit" (1:295), he finds that her words "didn't make her affect him any the less as a creature compounded of the finest elements; brilliant, delicate, complicated, but complicated with something divine." Even after Hyacinth is convinced of her deep entanglement in the revolution, "his imagination represented her . . . in places where a barrier of dazzling light shut her out from access or even from any appeal. He saw her with other people, in splendid rooms where 'the dukes' had possession of her, smiling, satisfied, surrounded, covered with jewels" (2:152).

Before his trip to the continent, Hyacinth's two idealized roles hover in his mind in a delicate balance. By the time he writes to the Princess from Venice, however, he feels an overwhelming need to escape the revolutionary part he has agreed to enact. Like James, he has come to understand that the entire "fabric of civilization" is based upon "the despotisms, the cruelties, the exclusions, the monopolies and the rapacities of the past" (2:145), and that to destroy the class structure that upholds art and culture would be to destroy art and culture themselves. He realizes that beauty is often the residue of mass misery, but thinks with greater horror of a society that "would cut up the ceilings of the Veronese into strips, so that everyone might have a little piece" (2:146).

The conflict between anarchy and art in *The Princess Casamassima* has been widely discussed, but James suggests, I think, an equally profound conflict between anarchy (or any radical form of egalitarianism) and love. Paul Muniment and the Princess are incapable of genuine affection because, in reducing all men to a common denominator, they overlook most of the distinguishing moral and social traits upon which personal love depends. To recognize no inherent distinctions in personal worth is, ultimately, to love everyone equally—or, more appropriately, to love no one. Like D. H. Lawrence, James insisted that love is an altogether private matter, and he realized that, when it is made democratic and communal, it ceases to exist. Romantic love, in particular, as Denis de Rougemont has observed, thrives upon the obstacles that separate lovers, obstacles such as class, race, religion, and nationality. Hyacinth's devotion to the Princess is a paradigm of this type of love. To remove all social barriers, as Muniment and his followers propose, would be to eliminate the grand struggle that both inspires and individualizes so many love affairs. The implications of a homogeneous society were even more devastating for James, who believed that love always involves man's desire to define his identity in relation to something distinct from himself. James must have recognized that a classless civilization would destroy (at least in the social sense) the self-defining potential of love.

The ultimate crisis that Hyacinth faces is that he is forced to choose between two kinds of self-destruction—he must kill either his ideal identity or himself. He realizes that to assist in the overthrow of the upper class by assassinating the duke would be to violate his deepest sense of self, to destroy his fondest self-conception. In his superb essay on *The Princess*, Lionel Trilling describes Hyacinth as a tragic hero of our civilization, "embodying two ideals at once" and accepting "the guilt of each."[12] Although Trilling is right in observing that Hyacinth's mind is in "a perfect equilibrium of *awareness*," his assumption that the suicide results wholly from an irresolvable ideological conflict hinges upon the assumption that Hyacinth is unable to *choose* between anarchy and art. Actually, by the time he returns from the continent he has made his choice: he wishes to preserve the European social order. More important, he has come to think of himself as an aristocrat, in spirit, if not in fact. The political crisis in Hyacinth's life is really an outgrowth of his fragmented personality, which he seeks to integrate through group identification and idealized love. Hyacinth is tormented, not because he is intellectually unable to decide, but because he has committed himself to one role while he desires another. Thus, when he receives his death summons, he realizes, like Isabel Archer, that he must play a public part that is utterly inimical to his deepest ideal of self. Isabel chooses to perform; Hyacinth chooses to die. There are other factors at work, however.

Hyacinth's self-destruction is brought on not simply by his awareness that he cannot live up to an ideal of self, but by his discovery that the ideal itself has been a delusion. He realizes, in short, that the Princess who had inspired his vision of himself is a fraud. He has believed so deeply both in her love and in her ultimate allegiance to the upper class that he imagined, in his moment of crisis, she would "engage to save him—to fling a cloud about him as [had] the goddess-mother of the Trojan hero" (2:127). He finds, instead, that she is willing to sacrifice him to a movement in which she cannot really believe. She is, in the end, the same consummate actress she had been in *Roderick Hudson*, only grown wearier and less passionate.[13] For self-amusement, she slips from pose to pose in a society whose greatest fault, in her eyes, is its dullness. Hyacinth can find no lasting identity in relation to the Princess because she possesses none herself. With her unconvincing attempts at living in poverty and her specious cant about political upheaval, she is an insincere socialist, yet, with her disrespect for the highest tastes and manners of Western culture, she is a false aristocrat.

But, if the Princess does not embody aristocracy, then who does? The answer that James suggests, and that Hyacinth seems to realize, is that no one does—or at least no one will in the future. Although James closes his novel with an obscure bookbinder's suicide, he simultaneously opens before us an apocalyptic vision of revolutionary violence. He composed *The Princess Casamassima* not only with a consciousness of Marx, but, as Trilling has noted, with a full awareness of the anarchist activities of his own day.[14] In 1886, the year the novel was published, James wrote to Charles Eliot Norton that the condition of the British upper class "seems to me in many ways very much the same rotten and collapsible one as that of the French aristocracy before the revolution . . . or perhaps it's more like the heavy, congested and depraved Roman world upon which the barbarians came down. . . ."[15] James had always felt a sense of helplessness before the colossal tides of political and social change. Years before, in a letter to another friend, he had described himself as a helpless passenger on "the locomotive of history," who wished only to "hang on" during the ride. By the end of *The Princess Casamassima*, the locomotive has gone out of control. James seems to be saying that the historical forces that shape society are scarcely more orderly or stable than those that shape our private impressions from moment to moment. Identity, it follows, is no less transient and elusive in a social sense than in a psychological sense.

When Hyacinth is no longer able to believe in the permanence of himself, the Princess, and the society around him, he comes to know the full horror of one who is cut off from both the world of his perceptions and his own past. On the eve of his suicide, he thinks of his relationship to the Princess, which had once governed his life, with "a strange, detached curiosity—strange and detached because everything else of his past had been engulfed in the abyss that opened before him . . ." (2:396). It was not many years before a similar abyss of isolation and confusion opened in James' life—and it is in this gulf of subjective entrapment that so many of his novels of the 1890s open and close.

FOUR

The Disturbed Midnight: Love and Solipsism in James' Fiction, 1895-1901

The self's a fine and private place
But none I think do there embrace.
F. W. DUPEE on the art of Henry James

IN LATE 1900, Henry James wrote to his friend Morton Fullerton of the "port" from which his life and work had taken sail:

> The port from which I set out was, I think, that of *the essential loneliness of my life*—and it seems to be the port also, in sooth, to which my course again finally directs itself! This loneliness (since I mention it)—what is it still but the deepest thing about one? Deeper about *me*, at any rate, than anything else; deeper than my "genius," deeper than my discipline, deeper than my pride, deeper, above all, than the deep counterminings of art.[1]

When James wrote this letter, he had just completed his drafts of *The Sacred Fount*—that bewildering, solipsistic "flight into the high fantastic"[2] that marks the end of a feverish decade of stories and novels that progressively illustrate "the essential loneliness" of the individual. For James, it was a decade characterized by a growing sense of alienation from his audience. This separation had begun in 1890 with the popular and critical failure of *The Tragic Muse*, a failure that led James to repudiate the novel form and seek the popular recognition he longed for in short stories and drama. The stories failed to generate popular interest, and, by the beginning of 1895, *Guy Domville* and its author had been hissed off the London stage by an audience that James could describe only as "a set of savages."[3] Swearing an oath "never again to have anything to do with a business which lets one into such traps, abysses and heartbreak,"[4] James embarked upon a six-year period of unprecedented creative activity, during which he produced three full-length novels, four novellas, and twenty-one short stories. Still, in the midst of this energetic output, after the publication of *The Awkward Age*, he could confide his inner misery to a young friend: "My books make no more sound or ripple than if I dropped them one after the other into the mud."[5]

As the turn of the century approached, James found himself not only without an audience, but bereft of many of the friends whose lives had given security, continuity, and stability to his own. The twelve years that passed since he had begun *The Tragic Muse* brought the deaths of two of James' most vital contacts with his childhood and American past, his sister Alice and his beloved aunt Catherine Walsh, four of his oldest and most cherished acquaintances, Lizzie Boott, Constance Fenimore Woolson, James Russell Lowell, and Robert Louis Stevenson, and his three closest London friends, George du Maurier, Fanny Kemble, and Mrs. Mahlon Sands. The loss of this last trio, in particular, seemed to James to augur a greater death: the collapse of the entire European social order. By the mid-nineties the fragile, beautiful, aesthetic world that James had chosen as his own seemed to totter on the edge of a dark abyss. The invasion of unparalleled troops of vulgar American tourists—the Sarah and Jim Pococks of his fiction—aroused in him a premonition of "the chaos or cataclysm toward which the whole thing is drifting." As a transplanted Yankee, James' horror was especially acute because the fellow countrymen who swarmed around him seemed to threaten and contaminate his American identity. To look at them was to see his own heritage and national character distorted, as if reflected in a circus glass. In a notebook entry of 1895, he describes the breakdown of the European world in a headlong rush of images, an imagery of flux that was becoming more and more prevalent in his fiction: ". . . the deluge of people, the insane movement for movement, the ruin of thought, of life, the negation of work, of literature, the swelling, roaring crowds, the 'where are you going?,' the age of Mrs. Jack, the figure of Mrs. Jack, the American, the nightmare—the *individual consciousness*—the mad ghastly climax or denouement."[6] During the winter of 1897, James fled from London and, after signing a twenty-one-year lease, sequestered himself at Lamb House in Rye.

The mellow old world of London society was dead to James—as dead as the America of his youth—and he could but stare out with fear and wonderment at the new, frantic, cosmopolitan generation that had sprung up. Under these conditions, James found it impossible to return to the international theme; he had lost contact with the new Daisy Millers and Christopher Newmans who strode ubiquitously through Hyde Park and Picadilly Circus. There was simply nothing exceptional any more about a young American in Europe. There remained for James only his naked "individual consciousness," isolated and bereft of all illusions of order. "You are not isolated," he had written to Grace Norton, who was suffering from extreme emotional depression in 1883; although life seemed only a chaos of "darkness," the novelist had urged his friend: "Don't melt too much into the universe, but be as solid and dense and fixed as you can."[7] Although James could not name it at the time, he sensed "something" in life "that holds one in one's place, makes it a standpoint in the universe which it is probably good not to foresake." In James' fiction, as we have seen, this "something" that gives a sense of fixity to one's identity is the love of man and woman—in his life, it was the love that we call friendship. Seventeen years after his letter to Grace Norton, James sought the comfort that he had then provided. Looking ahead to the gathering "grey years" and feeling "the steady swift movement of the ebb of the great tide," he implores Fullerton: "Hold me then *you* with any squeeze; grip me with any grip; press me with any pressure; trust me with any trust."[8] For James, however, the only sense of order possible in his solitude came, paradoxically, through dialogues with his own mind, through the struggle and madness of artistic creation.

James' preoccupation during the late 1890s with matters of point of view and form—a preoccupation that appears at times to border upon obsession—is not so much a novelist's interest in literary style as a man's response to the horror of self-entrapment. For

Maisie, the governess of *The Turn of the Screw*, the telegraphist of *In the Cage*, each of the characters in *The Awkward Age*, and the unnamed narrator of *The Sacred Fount*, reality consists of nothing more than what is seen from the point of view of subjective consciousness. Each is enclosed within the airtight world of his own perceptions, a world that, Pater had written, lay inside "that thick wall of personality through which no real voice has ever pierced"[9] and that F. H. Bradley would later term "the closed sphere." Since nothing from outside penetrates the all-enclosing dome of consciousness, everything within the range of perception is part of the perceiver; there is no objective boundary, no fixed otherness to define the limits of individual being. Within this dome, the unanchored individual floats in the immeasurable sea of his own impressions, impressions that ebb and flow without rhythm or regularity. With nothing inside or outside of the mind to give shape or fixity, individual identity becomes nothing more than the ever-changing sum of consciousness. From moment to moment, the individual melts into the phosphorescent foam of his own impressions, melts out of one self and into another. In his own isolation, James came to believe that the only order or stability that could possibly exist within the perceiving self or the world of its impressions was that which the imagination created. His belabored attention to the intricacies of form in his novels of the late 1890s, his fascination with the geometric arrangement of chapters, his proclivity for welding words into long, elaborately linked chains, his consistent focus upon a single point of view, and the uncharacteristic brevity of these works were all a part of James' strategy for creating an imaginative realm of order in his art.

The paradox inherent in most of his works around the turn of the century is that although their theme is, generally stated, the chaos of individual consciousness, the fictional form that encloses this theme has the fragile, crystalline precision of a cut glass bowl. This peculiar conflict between form and meaning reflects James' ambivalence toward his own isolation: he recognized the terror of human solitude and addressed the problem more directly than ever before, yet this very obsession transported him farther and farther from the world of men and things, deeper and deeper into the sphere of his own mind. The very act of writing itself seemed to contribute to this alienation: when an arthritic condition in his right hand forced James to engage a stenographer in 1897, he found himself removed from even the palpable pen and paper with which he created. Like Eliot's Prufrock, James could think of himself as a kind of disembodied voice. Through dictation, he complained to a friend: "I can address you only through an embroidered veil of sound."[10] For James, consciousness itself was filtered through a sort of "embroidered veil," an all-enclosing transparent medium that forever separated the individual viewer from a world of impressions that he could see but never really touch. Desmond MacCarthy recalls James' psychological isolation when, as a young admirer, he spoke with him shortly after the turn of the century:

> But an incident comes back to me as revealing something much deeper in [James]. . . . It occurred after a luncheon party of which he had been, as they say, "the life." We happened to be drinking our coffee together while the rest of the party had moved on the verandah. "What a charming picture they make," he said, with his great head aslant, "the women there with their embroidery, the. . . ." There was nothing in his words, anybody might have spoken them; but in his attitude, in his voice, in his whole being at the moment, I divined such complete detachment, that I was startled into speaking out of myself: "I can't bear to look at life like that," I blurted out, "I want to be in everything. Perhaps that is why I cannot *write*, it makes me feel absolutely alone. . . ." The effect of this confession upon him was instantaneous and surprising. He leant forward and grasped my arm excitedly: "Yes, it's solitude. If it runs after you and catches you, well and good. But for heaven's sake don't run after *it*. It is absolute solitude." He got up hurriedly and joined the others.[11]

As he approached old age, James found that the conscious mind that, in his childhood, loved nothing more than composing the raw material of experience into "the cherished scene," had evolved to a condition in which it could see life as nothing more than a series of detached, evanescent "pictures." Realizing that these ordered pictures were mere illusions arranged by the mind of a perceiving artist, he knew that order within the self—the illusion of a stable, integrated identity—was possible only if the imagination could hold fast in its relation to a single picture, a single frame on the continuous reel of experience. In the "great relation" of love—the relation to which James perpetually addressed himself—a sense of identity was possible only if the changing beloved could be transformed into an unchanging image.

In the Cage, a brilliant but frequently overlooked novella written in 1898, presents James' most appropriate metaphor for the prison of consciousness within which romantic love must operate in his fiction of the nineties: a telegraphist's booth with a barred window kaleidoscopically framing pictures of the passing world. If Isabel Archer, with her intense self-awareness but distorted vision of the world, is James' first major heroine to seek identity through love, the incurably imaginative telegraphist of In the Cage is one of the novelist's final elaborations upon this imperfect model of "consciousness." The telegraphist is James' most extreme version, to date, of an all-absorbing mind seeking to define its own limits through an imaginative love. Although the novella stretches well over one hundred pages, James carefully refrains from referring to his heroine as anything more specific than "the telegraphist." This title emphasizes not merely the girl's occupation, but the distinctive point of view as well that her occupation affords. In a world that is constantly dissolving and re-forming itself before her eyes, she is, from moment to moment, that which she sees from her particular vantage point. As in The Princess Casamassima—his only other sizable work dealing primarily with lower class life—James focuses upon a poor but sensitive individual's need to establish a point of fixity, an objective frame of reference in the world of flux. Like Hyacinth Robinson, who is never quite sure whether he is an aristocrat or a proletarian, the little telegraphist is extremely confused about her role in life. Disdaining all classes of society for their pettiness and stupidity, she sees no logical relationship between her own intellectual superiority and the economic state to which fate has reduced her. Although she knows that she can never enter the "grande monde," she believes that she holds secret membership in a kind of aristocracy of fine minds. It is by virtue of this subtle membership that she dreams of establishing her identity in some immediate relation to a member of the upper class.

The economic collapse of the telegraphist's family and subsequent years of poverty have schooled her in a knowledge that few of James' other heroines possess. Although, like Isabel Archer, she voraciously reads "borrowed novels, very greasy, in fine print," she turns to literature, not to corroborate her sense of life, but to escape from it.[12] She shares none of Isabel's or Daisy's illusions of life as a well-ordered romance. Viewing the world from the telegraph window, "she set finally down to the safe proposition that the outside element was 'changeable' " (p. 206). James reinforces the telegraphist's vision of the world as fluid by letting the imagery of water wash onto every page of his story. The girl thinks of the people who pass her window as fish who "swam straight away [and] lost themselves in the bottomless common" (p. 190), and imagines her family as "submerged, floundering, panting, swimming for their lives" (p. 191). She is no less skeptical of metaphysical absolutes, determining at an early age that "real justice was not in the world." Isabel had sought to satisfy her unique need for self-definition through her love for Osmond—but she believed her love-image to be real. The telegraphist, by contrast, knows that human personality, like the external world, is a plastic element that can never be comprehended in a single impression. She realizes, therefore, that any lover who is to provide the relational identity she seeks must be the creation of her imagination. Like many of Conrad's characters, she understands that order, permanence, and identity itself are illusions that man requires to go on living. The telegraphist's dilemma is essentially that which inspired the pragmatic philosophy of James' brother, William; she is torn between a need to believe in some objectified truth in the universe and a skeptical intelligence that seems to preclude belief in anything. Eight years after *In the Cage*, William wrote that "the true is the name of whatever proves itself to be good in the way of belief, and good, too, for definite, assignable reasons."[13] Although Henry could write to William in 1907 of "the wonder of the extent to which all my life I have . . . unconsciously pragmatised,"[14] he had already created fictional worlds in which William's conception of truth as a synthetic process of discovery was simply inoperative, worlds in which "what is better for us to believe," and "what is true for us"[15] are not the same. The only "good" that the telegraphist knows comes, not through the open pursuit of truth, but through her fantasizing imagination and her willful suspension of disbelief. Far from having "definite assignable reasons" for believing in the imaginary characters she creates, she enjoys a "moral holiday" only when she abandons rational knowledge altogether. By 1898, James had reached that bleak pole of awareness at which willful self-deception becomes man's only pragmatic choice.

The telegraph cage, then, is not merely a window of subjective perception, but a studio for self-conscious artistic creation. Behind her bars, the telegraphist catches only desultory snatches of conversation, glimpses of passing faces, and cryptic messages from representatives of the great world. Yet, from these disconnected threads of impressions, she weaves a vast tapestry in her imagination. She endows faces with personalities and histories and constructs elaborate stories around the telegrams that she receives. "What she could handle freely, she said to herself, was combinations of men and women. The only weakness in her faculty came from the positive abundance of her contact with the human herd" (p. 178). The task of distilling order out of chaos that the telegraphist, as artist of life, faces, is almost identical to that which the novelist confronts. James' explanation of his own role in his preface to *Roderick Hudson* may be fruitfully applied to several of his characters. "Really, universally, relations stop nowhere, and the exquisite problem of the artist is eternally but to draw, by a geometry of his own, the circle within which they shall happily *appear* to do so."[16] Presumably, if the sensitive mind pursues any set of relations too far, studies any concatenation of circumstances too closely, it will become lost in a vast inscrutable network. In order to create the illusion of order, therefore, the artist must maintain a certain distance from life, the raw material of his creation; he must have what the telegraphist calls "a margin." Clearly, the telegraphist's self-imposed margin from chaos is her cage. From this vantage point, she can transform Captain Everard into the desperate, love-crazed Lothario whom she longs to serve. Like Isabel, she believes that her ideal identity lies in selfless servitude and vicarious experience. For the telegraphist, however, the role of confidante, of listener rather than actor, is the only one compatible with her knowledge of the insubstantiality of human personality.

The telegraphist, like her American cousin, falls in love with an image of her inamorato before she ever sees him. So keenly is the girl's fantasy life attuned to the sensory world, that she needs but a whiff of expensive perfume, a beautiful face, and an enigmatic telegram to conjure up a vivid scenario. "She would know the hand again any time. It was as handsome and as everything else as the woman herself. The woman herself had, on learning of his flight, pushed past Everard's servant and into his room; she had written her missive at his table with his pen. All this, every inch of it, came through in the waft she blew through and left behind her" (p. 182). Later, having glimpsed Everard for a moment, the telegraphist begins "seeing him in imagination at other places and with other girls" (p. 206). Next, by willing herself to believe in her fixed image of the man, she creates an auxiliary image of herself as his devotee. Finally, she begins to imagine that Everard not only notices her attention, but comes to depend upon it, that an unspoken spiritual bond has formed between them. She nourishes a belief in "the divine chance of his consciously liking her," and fancies that, in the midst of his woes, "her own eyes struck him . . . as the one pitying pair in the crowd" (p. 208). It is at this point that James' heroine ceases to be a self-conscious dreamer and commits the sin of artistic hubris—she believes that her creation has become real. *In the Cage* is James' vision of the artistic imagination gone wild, and, in the telegraphist's self-deception, one finds an implicit warning to those who would take the "geometry" of their art for the true shape of life. Driven by love to make her fantasy come alive, the telegraphist takes her first trembling steps from the cage, thus eliminating the requisite distance between herself and the world of flux. Meeting Everard by a calculated accident one evening, she is crushed to discover how little the handsome gentleman understands the delicate relationship she has fantasized. When she asks him if he senses something "wonderful" in their association, he expresses his gratitude, not for her devotion as a spiritual guardian, but for her efficiency as a public servant. The girl's sudden realization that Everard is not the responsive soulmate she had imagined destroys not only her image of him, but of herself. "She maintained her fixed smile a moment and turned her eyes over the peopled darkness, unconfused now, because there was something much more confusing. This, with a great fatal rush, was simply the fact that they were thus together . . . She stared straight away in silence till she felt she looked an idiot; then, to say something, to say nothing, she attempted a sound which ended in a flood of tears" (p. 221). Stripped of her identity, the telegraphist can but openly declare her love and retreat again to the security of her cage.

Although she can never recapture her vision of Everard as a partner in spirit, her image of him as a passionate but persecuted lover remains unshattered. It is, in fact, his very insensitivity that allows her to conceive of herself, in a slightly modified role, as an utterly disinterested, long-suffering servant. The telegraphist derives a great deal of moral self-gratification from this image of herself, and it is, therefore, fitting that her one great act of self-sacrifice should finally contribute to so meretricious a cause. Having "saved" Everard by reciting to him the contents of an old telegram, the girl discovers from a friend that the rich, dashing, abused suitor of her imagination was really a poor, ruthless fortune hunter. The information that she supplied has merely gone to make him rich. The novella ends with the disillusioned telegraphist gazing into Paddington Canal at the eternal element of flux and determining to marry her patient fiancé immediately. The "little home" into which she plans to retreat is a cage that will afford no view. The telegraphist, having learned to fear her own inability to distinguish illusion from reality, willfully commits her imagination to the exile of a life with Mr. Mudge. As in *The Portrait of a Lady*, marriage ultimately represents the reduction of a free, spontaneous spirit to a constricting social form. By the time James wrote *In the Cage*, however, what his heroine came to fear most was not the enslavement of her imagination, but, rather, its freedom. Unable to discover the boundaries between her unstable imagination and an equally unstable universe, the telegraphist seeks to escape "the ordeal of consciousness" through a withdrawal from all external sources of psychic stimulation.

Having given up the vertiginous world of London for the solitude of Rye, James painfully understood the telegraphist's need for withdrawal. It is a need that preoccupies many of his characters of the 1890s—that period of literary decadence that he termed "the disturbed midnight of our actual literature."[17] In his satirical portrait of Gabriel Nash, the brilliant but futile dilettante of *The Tragic Muse* (1890), who gives up the labor necessary for artistic creation because he thinks that it vulgarizes his personal style, James had revealed a thorough disapproval of Wildean aestheticism.[18] One must never withdraw from the sources of life, James seemed to be saying, never repudiate the human scene with all of its complexities, never forget that art should communicate, never cease the "doing" necessary for artistic achievement. James had always felt a personal distaste for Wilde, whom he considered frivolous, self-indulgent, and artistically "lazy," and, by 1894, he came to view "faint, pale, embarrassed, exquisite Pater" in much the same light.[19] James saw him as a creature who dwelt so thoroughly in an aesthetic realm that he existed for others only as a literary voice; he seemed a "pen" more than a person, a "mask without the face." Although the personal life-styles of Wilde and Pater could have scarcely been more different, James realized that both the London dandy and the Oxford recluse had withdrawn into a private world of subtle artistic sensations, and that both cultivated these sensations at the expense of human relationships and literary productivity. Despite his aversion to the aestheticism of the nineties, however, the stories and novels that James wrote during this same period reveal his own fascination with retreating into a rarified, hermetical sphere of being. Mrs. Gereth sequesters herself amid the antique splendors of her beloved Poynton; George Dane, oppressed by stacks of unfinished paperwork, dreams himself into a world of peaceful inactivity, a "great good place" beyond; and Ralph Pendrel, driven by his "sense of the past," retreats through an old portrait into the world of early nineteenth-century England.[20] The years between 1895 and 1901 were truly "the disturbed midnight" of James' own literature, but, unlike Pater, Huysmans, and Wilde, whose creative outputs are slight, James never abjured the labor of creating and gave himself entirely to passive aesthetic enjoyment. Although the novelist was tempted by the idea of enervated isolation, he was tempted for the very opposite reason that the aesthetes were. The "other world" that lures his characters—but to which James himself never fully succumbs—is not a place of exquisite sensory stimulation, not the Paterean realm of "strange dyes, strange colors, and curious odors," but a static void where one ceases to be conscious of the flow of impressions altogether. Unlike James, the aesthetes celebrated the entropic chaos of consciousness and the impermanence of individual identity. For Wilde, who wished always to "multiply personality," and for Pater, who, passing "swiftly from point to point," rejoiced in "that strange, perpetual, weaving and unweaving of ourselves,"[21] the whirlpool of private consciousness could scarcely spin fast enough. But who could take pleasure in this kind of refined solipsism for an entire lifetime? What human being, at some point, has not longed for unity of being and for contact with some other individual? James had never been able to ignore these questions or to tolerate an aesthetic that did, but in the dim nightfall of the late 1890s, he saw only one escape from the chaos of the self—the radical diminution of psychic awareness.

In the stories and novels that immediately follow *In the Cage*, James continually asks how or where one might escape consciousness. Even as he searches for an outlet, however, he persistently addresses an even larger question: is the curse of self-awareness by which we know ourselves to be merely shifting swarms of impressions preferable to not knowing? Since full consciousness entails a submission to the eddies of experience and an acceptance of life's chaos, the dilemma of knowing or not knowing reduced itself, for James, to the fundamental question, "to be or not to be." *The Awkward Age*, which he began almost immediately upon completion of *In the Cage* in September of 1898, explores the two possible states of being in which time and change do not exist and in which identity seems stable. In the world of the novel, Aggie and Mr. Longdon stand as fixed poles; the former is a preconscious child whose self-awareness has yet to be born, the latter, an old man who dwells almost exclusively in the dead past. For Longdon, who worships the image of his dead lover, Lady Julia, the clock has stopped, for Aggie, who is loved *as* an image of eternal innocence, it has yet to start. Whereas Longdon has defined— one might almost say "mummified"—his identity through his love of the dead, Aggie, because she is not yet a conscious human being, but only an image, allows others to define their identities in relation to her. As visions in an artist's imagination, these characters might reside eternally in a kind of time lock, but James knew that, in real life, neither the aging man nor the little girl could remain unchanged forever; Mr. Longdon must strive to bring Lady Julia back to life in the world of time; "little Aggie" must grow up.

James' obsession with time in *The Awkward Age* arose from his awareness that temporal flux destroys not only identity, but eventually life itself. In a letter to Henrietta Reubell of 1899, he describes the novel and then goes on to remark: ". . . I like growing (that is I like, for many reasons, *being*) old: 56! But I don't like growing *older*. I quite love my present age and the compensations, simplifications, freedom, independences, memories, advantages of it. But I don't keep it long enough—it passes too quickly."[22] In many ways, Longdon, who at fifty-five has "doubled the Cape of years," is James' fictional alter ego. James was fifty-five himself when he began the novel, a lifelong bachelor, like Longdon, living alone in a house in the country. If Longdon has his Lady Julia, James had the memory of Minny Temple, and, if the new generation that had sprung up in London appalls Longdon, it is because it appalled his creator. There is one crucial distinction, however, that finally saves James from a morbid identification with his character. Longdon has lived entirely in the past for thirty years, and James fully recognizes that this kind of existence is a death in life. His initiation into the warm life bath of Buckingham Crescent is appropriately figured forth as a resurrection from the dead. After a dinner party at Mrs. Brook's, he confesses to Vanderbank, "There have been things this evening that make me feel as if I had been disinterred—literally dug up from a long sleep."[23] Longdon later compares himself to "Rip van Winkle" and finds that, upon re-entering London, he is "really quite mouldy" (p. 4). "I'm old-fashioned and narrow and ignorant," he truthfully adds, "I've lived for years in a hole" (p. 35).

Longdon's sufficient "hole" is a country house filled with "portraits of women dead" and furnishings that suggest "everywhere . . . the tone of old red surfaces, the style of old white facings, the age of old high creepers, the long confirmation of time" (p. 336). Like Dickens' Miss Havisham, who wears the yellowed bridal gown in which she was to be married and lives amid the mouldering decorations of a wedding feast, Longdon inhabits the world he knew when his lover rejected him. After Lady Julia declined his marriage proposal, thirty years before the opening of the novel, Longdon's life "took a form"—a form governed by an almost religious worship of the memory of his beloved. Longdon was free to marry after his rejection, but, in imagined deference to Lady Julia, he chose a life of self-imposed celibacy and silent adoration before her altar. "The better a woman is," he tells Vanderbank, ". . . the more she enjoys in a quiet way some fellow's having been rather bad, rather dark and desperate, about her—for her. I dare say, I mean, that though Lady Julia insisted that I ought to marry she wouldn't have liked it much if I had" (pp. 33-34). With Lady Julia in the grave, Longdon may impute any desire to her that he wishes—including his own. Like any worshiper, he needs to believe that the object of his adoration somehow compels and appreciates his attendance. In truth, however, Longdon is motivated, not by Lady Julia's desire for his service, but by his own need to serve. His devotion, like the telegraphist's, is finally not selfless, but self-serving; he loves not simply Lady Julia, but the role, the identity that she provides for him. Nanda recognizes a kind of psychological possessiveness in her friend when she remarks: "You feel as if my grandmother were quite *your* property" (p. 153). Longdon's memory of Lady Julia allows him to live in the past—a life that, as Mrs. Brook tells him, has a unique advantage: ". . . the past is the one thing beyond all spoiling: there it is, don't you think?—to speak for itself—and, if need be, only *of* itself" (p. 191). Since Lady Julia is dead and beyond change, Longdon can stand perpetually in relation to her as a ministrant. His identity, which was initially forged in the fire of his love, will endure as long as an immaculate image of her continues to glow in his mind. For Longdon, however, this image alone is finally not enough; like an aging Pygmalion, he longs to bring Lady Julia to life in the world of flesh and blood.

Although James is never explicit about why this introverted bachelor emerges from hibernation in his mid-fifties, it is probable that Longdon feels able to enter the world of time because he believes his identity, at last, to be timeless. At fifty-five, he is too old to be a sexual lover—he is compelled to love Lady Julia's reincarnation in the same spirit of chaste adoration in which he loves her dead image.[24] His role in society, therefore, is essentially the same as his role in solitude. When Mitchy asks him if he has come to London in pursuit of some "lady in her millions," Longdon explains, "I'm afraid 'pursuit,' with me, is over." What remains at Longdon's age is the less treacherous pastime of detached "observation." His detachment, however, is measured, not in distance, but in time; he habitually perceives the world of the present through a telescope of the past. Thus, when Vanderbank shows him Nanda's portrait, he makes the rather macabre observation that she "has just Lady Julia's expression. . . . She's much more like the dead than like the living" (p. 24). It is appropriate that

CHAPTER FOUR

Longdon encounters Nanda first as a picture, because, for much of the novel, he sees her as little more than the living image of a dead ghost. When Vanderbank asks him if the "little girls" of his own day gave their portraits to young men, he replies with something between "superiority and regret," "They never did to me" (p. 17). In Longdon's imagination, Nanda will become that portrait of Lady Julia that he never received.

Despite his sense of the past, however, Longdon is gradually forced to realize that, unlike the dead portraits that hang at his estate, the living ones at Buckingham Crescent are wont to step out of their frames. Awakening into the world of other human beings, into the world of flux, he finds that he has "lost the link" in his sleep. He is astonished at a society in which adultery is a conversational topic of consuming interest, infamous French novels circulate from one drawing room to another, young men stay up all night smoking cigarettes, young ladies make gifts of their pictures, and, worst of all, "declare their passion." If these practices fail to bring a blush to the cheek of a certain young person in the novel, they succeed in reddening Longdon's wrinkled face. He is quick to realize that, if Nanda is to remain the image of her uncorrupted grandmother, "the real old thing," she must be "got out . . . out of her mother's house."

What terrifies Longdon most about Mrs. Brook's world is not so much that it has changed, as that its inhabitants are constantly changing. For Mrs. Brook, Vanderbank, and Mitchy, life is a matter of pure experiential flux; their behavior is governed neither by traditional social forms nor by moral absolutes. To "freely surrender to the play of perception," to "take things in at the pores" is to be fully conscious in the world of Buckingham Crescent; and to be fully conscious is to realize that all values and all experiences are relative. Since nothing has truth outside the individual mind, it is, as Van suggests, "impossible to say too much" about anything— "it's impossible to say enough" (p. 20). Reality exists only as subjective perception, and our perception changes from moment to moment. Even Nanda finally comes to realize that, in full consciousness, "one become[s] a sort of little drain-pipe with everything flowing through" (p. 358). Mitchy tells her that a more appropriate metaphor would be "a little aeolian-harp set in the drawing-room window and vibrating in the breeze of conversation." Although this model is more appealing, it is not quite accurate. Unlike the harp, which gives form to the passing breeze by translating it into music, there is no arrangement to what naturally passes through the individual consciousness. More important, as Nanda is quick to point out, "the harp gives out a sound, and we—at least we try to—give out none." Like water flowing through a drainpipe, their fleeting impressions are enclosed within the impenetrable wall of the individual mind; there is no common sound, no shared perception. For all their prodigious conversation, their claims of solidarity, and attempts to become "conscious of one another," the inhabitants of Mrs. Brook's circle remain solipsists. They see themselves "reflected" in each other, but neither the mirror nor its reflection has any reality beyond the subjective mind. Further, since these self-reflections are evanescent, they cannot provide even the illusion of a fixed identity. A decade after the publication of *The Awkward Age*, the parlor world that James' characters inhabit will become that of T. S. Eliot's early poetry, a realm peopled by phantoms and bounded by the human skull, in which one "must borrow every changing shape to find expression."[25]

The peculiar structure of James' novel reinforces, at every point, our sense of psychological isolation and the impermanence of identity. The book's form is, as James says, "all dramatic and scenic,"[26] and, in each of his ten "scenes," his characters give a temporary form to themselves by adopting a role. For the first time, in *The Awkward Age*, we find none of James' characteristic "going behind"; there is no longer any attempt to lay bare the psyche of a character or to trace the vague contours of an inner self. Buckingham Crescent is not the world as an omnipresent novelist imagines it from above, but the swirling, fragmented world of appearances that we experience in life. To live in the society of men, James realized, is to borrow any changing shape that the situation demands, to be perpetually formed and re-formed by experience. Vanderbank admits that "there isn't anything anyone can say that I won't agree to" (p. 20), and the mercurial Mitchy, with almost no "intrinsic appearance," is so adaptable and self-effacing as to seem "a kind of monster of benevolence." Just as each section or "scene" in the novel is a self-contained entity, each character, for whom these sections are named, constitutes a world unto himself. With no principle of identity within or outside themselves, they are, as Mitchy explains in a moment of insight, "simply a collection of natural affinities . . . meeting perhaps principally in Mrs. Brook's drawing-room—though sometimes also in old Van's . . . sometimes even in mine—governed at any rate everywhere by Mrs. Brook, in our mysterious ebbs and flows, very much as the tides are governed by the moon" (p. 124).

If Mrs. Brook changes phases rather more frequently than her lunar counterpart, there is a fixed star that twinkles faintly beyond the fringe of the spinning social galaxy—little Aggie. Just as Longdon has preserved Lady Julia's image within the crystalline walls of his imagination, little Aggie has been preserved as a living image of innocence by her Aunt Jane. Nanda becomes a portrait of the past in Longdon's eyes, but Aggie is "the real old thing itself." Raised in an Italian convent, in accordance with time-honored European tradition, and sheltered from the corrupting influences of adult society, she remains, at seventeen, "as slight and white, as delicately lovely, as a gathered garden lily" (p. 93). Unlike Longdon, who is merely stuck in time, Aggie is scarcely conscious that time exists. She is James' purest version of Emerson's "eyeball"—impressions pour through her mind like rays of light through a window, leaving almost no trace in her memory. Since past experiences have no meaning for Aggie, she has no sense of who she has been. Her identity remains essentially fixed for seventeen years because she lives in a perpetual present; memory and thought association—the processes that give rise to self-consciousness—have hardly begun. Unlike Nanda, who is the innocent victim of a consciousness that is "almost indecorously active," Aggie is pre-conscious innocence, the Lockean "tabula rasa." "On little Aggie's slate the figures were yet to be written;

which sufficiently accounted for the difference of the two surfaces. Both the girls [were] as lambs with the great shambles of life in their future; but while one, with its neck in a pink ribbon, had no consciousness but that of being fed from the hand with the small sweet biscuit of unobjectionable knowledge, the other struggled with instincts and forebodings, with the suspicion of its doom and far-borne scent, in the flowery fields, of blood" (p. 239). Although Aggie has a face "formed to express everything," all of "the elements of play . . . had nothing to play with." Nearly two decades before *The Awkward Age*, James had found something charming in Pansy Osmond's frail innocence, but, taking that innocence to its extremity, in Aggie, he raised the disturbing specter of an idiot child.

Poised between the chaos of Buckingham Crescent and the timeless realm of Aggie and Mr. Longdon is James' heroine, Nanda. Like her insuperable mother, Nanda is, by nature, "conscious and aware," cursed with a "hideous intelligence." Unlike Mrs. Brook, however, who insists that "one must be what one is"—meaning that one must accept the impermanence of personality—Nanda constantly longs to be that which she is not. If Mr. Longdon defines himself through the love of an image, Nanda wishes to *be* that image. As the waves of consciousness break upon her, she increasingly seeks to escape the burden of her awareness, to deny the temporal chaos and fragmentation that she senses. Her first and fondest desire is to look and be like little Aggie. She sees the girl as an embodiment of timeless innocence and tells Mitchy: "Now the beauty of Aggie is that she knows nothing—but absolutely, utterly the least little tittle of anything. . . . Ah, say what you will—it *is* the way we ought to be" (p. 356). Concomitant almost with the dawn of Nanda's self-awareness is her realization that she can never again return to Aggie's state of mindless purity—at best, she can only help to preserve that purity in others. When she meets Mr. Longdon, however, Nanda finds that, although she cannot become the Aggie-image of her own dream, she can, perhaps, become part of his. She falls in love with Longdon's image of her grandmother, and hopes that, with his support, she

CHAPTER FOUR

may become that image. "If [grandmother] had you," she tells him, "so I've got you too" (p. 230). The psychology of self-deception through which James' heroine strives to anchor her identity in the uncorrupted past is summed up best, perhaps, in Novalis' remark: "It is certain my conviction gains infinitely, the moment another soul will believe in it." In order to become the image of Lady Julia, Nanda needs only for Longdon to believe in her, and, in order for Longdon to believe in her, she need only be willing to believe in herself.

What is new and disturbing in James' treatment of love in *The Awkward Age* is that Nanda's quest for identity takes her beyond the image-love that is solipsism to a form that is overtly narcissistic. Even Longdon, in his necrophilia, worships the image of another, but the portrait that Nanda enshrines in her imagination is a portrait of herself. Nanda is, of course, also desperately in love with Vanderbank, but, as Dorothea Krook has pointed out, she loves him precisely because she knows that he is the only man, apart from Longdon, who could love her only as the pure image that she longs to be. Although Van is a member of Mrs. Brook's decadent menage, as a fallen aristocrat, he maintains an "heredi-tary prejudice" for girls of old-world innocence. Nanda can only "respect," as Mitchy puts it, "a man who would have minded" her fall from innocence, and, just as she had fortified Longdon's dream of Lady Julia with her own belief, she needs Van to believe in her vision of herself. Thus, in Nanda's imagination, he becomes a kind of mirror—a fixed image himself, reflecting a fixed image of her.

Unfortunately for Nanda, Van is the one character in the novel who can never see her simply as an image. "I've a fulcrum of sal-vation," he tells Longdon in the opening scene, "which consists of a deep consciousness and the absence of a rag of illusion" (p. 33). Van realizes that he can never love Nanda, certainly never marry her, because, through her acute understanding of the world, she has been "spoiled for him." From the outset of the novel, he senses that she has already acquired the wisdom of Eve in an un-Edenic Victorian world, and that, though she be pure of heart, she can never again be pure of mind. It is the singular paradox of Van's nature that, despite his ideal of innocence, he advocates a complete submission to the flux of experience and the development of full awareness for those who have already eaten of the tree of knowledge. This self-effacing young man, who seems at once to embrace a relativistic view of the world and to worship a moral absolute of innocence, is one of the most psychologically tortured and self-defeating characters in all of James' fiction. As a "modern man," he recognizes that personality has no more shape or solidity than the sensory impressions that form it, yet in his insistence upon perfect purity in a wife, "old Van" seems as antiquarian as Longdon and as naive as Nanda. What distinguishes Van from all of James' earlier creations, however, particularly from Nanda, Longdon, and the telegraphist, is that he never deludes himself about the possibility of his love-image becoming real—it remains for him always a purely imaginative conception. In clinging to an ideal of timeless innocence in the face of this knowledge, Van reaches that "final end of belief" that Wallace Stevens speaks of—the belief in a fiction that one knows to be only a fiction.

As vessels of consciousness, who long for an impossible image of purity, Van and Nanda are both doomed, as Mitchy puts it, "to love in vain." Van realizes this long before his young admirer, and, once he senses that she has fallen, he tries to lead her into full self-awareness. The course of their relationship becomes a psychic tug of war—while Nanda wishes to draw Van into a timeless realm in which he can love her, he tries to force her to live in the world of time. This struggle reaches its climax in a metaphysical exchange midway through the novel, when Nanda confides to Van her strange "fear" of him.

"My fear of you isn't superficial. I mean it isn't immediate—not of you just as you stand," she explained. "It's of some dreadfully possible future you."

"Well," said the young man, smiling down at her, "don't forget that if there's to be such a monster, there'll also be a future you, proportionately developed, to deal with him."

She had closed her parasol in the shade and her eyes attached themselves to the small hole she had dug in the ground with its point. "We shall both have moved, you mean?"

"It's charming to feel that we shall probably have moved together."

"Ah, if moving's changing," she returned, "there won't be much for me in that. I shall never change—I shall always be just the same. The same old mannered modern slangy hack," she continued quite gravely. "Mr. Longdon has made me feel that." . . .

"Yes," she pursued, "what I am I must remain. I haven't what's called a principle of growth" (pp. 213-214).

To recognize a change in Van, Nanda senses, would be to recognize the changes continually taking place within herself. The "dreadfully possible future" Van who frightens her is really a reflection of the dreadfully conscious future self that she anticipates. Although Nanda has, by this time, come to think of herself as a "modern slangy hack" and later apologizes to Longdon for not being more like her immaculate ancestor, she still thinks of her own identity as fixed and measures it against the unwavering image of her dead grandmother.

After their discussion, however, Nanda understands that, because Van expects her to mature, she can never be the kind of woman that he could wed. When Longdon importunes her to marry, she prophetically replies: "It's lovely of you to wish it, but I shall be one of the people who don't. I shall be at the end . . . one of those who haven't" (p. 232). Unable to believe any longer that she can become the image that she and Longdon love, Nanda is compelled to alter her relation to this ideal of innocence. If she cannot *be* Aggie or Lady Julia, she can at least, in Longdon's fashion, worship Aggie as an icon and serve at her shrine. Just as Longdon had tried to preserve Nanda by marrying her off to Van, Nanda tries to perpetuate Aggie's innocence—that is her ignorance—by yoking her to Mitchy. "Marry her," she entreats him, "beautifully, grandly save her . . . keep her from becoming like the Duchess . . . get her away—take her out of her aunt's life" (p. 355).

For all its appearance of selflessness, Nanda's matchmaking serves her own needs far more than Aggie's. "The thing that's important to one," she tells Mitchy, "is the thing one sees oneself, and it's quite enough if I see what can be made of that child." Nanda's remark may seem to echo Ralph Touchett, who lived "for the thrill of seeing" what life would make of Isabel Archer, but, by 1899, James had come to realize that vicarious love and "selfless" servitude are often masks for self-interest. He painfully understood that the desire to freeze another human being in a timeless image inevitably involves a desire to create an image of oneself. The beloved is reduced finally to the status of an object, to a kind of looking glass in which we see our idealized self steadily reflected. Whereas Ralph had wished to grant Isabel the greatest possible freedom and to watch the gradual refinement of her consciousness, Nanda, desperately wishing to define herself in relation to an image of absolute purity, seeks to preserve Aggie as a kind of ethereal butterfly within the glass prison of marriage. Mitchy, however, to whom she entrusts the key that could unlock Aggie's mind, proves a rather careless jailer. When we next see Aggie, shortly after her marriage, the "little lamb" whom Lady Jane had "tended and guarded," is playing a flirtatious game with her aunt's lover, Lord Petherton. Thrust abruptly into adult society, Aggie does not become acutely conscious, but simply vulgar; she shares in the immorality of Mrs. Brook's circle while partaking of none of its intelligence.

At the same time that Aggie's antics shatter Nanda's image of her, Nanda fractures her own image for Longdon. For this climactic scene, James assembles his entire cast at a party given by Nanda's friend, Tishy Grendon. Mrs. Brook, wishing to insure that her beloved Van will never marry her daughter, forces Nanda to publicly acknowledge that she has read a salacious French novel. Ironically, the revelation that Mrs. Brook so carefully arranges to shock Van merely corroborates what he has long suspected about Nanda. The only person genuinely stunned is Longdon, who bids his hostess a quick, ceremonious "Good night," and beats a hasty retreat to his country estate. What is most remarkable about Nanda's confession is that she uses the trap that her mother has set to bring about her own moral triumph. In openly acknowledging her fall from innocence, she not only forces Longdon to realize the impossibility of their shared dream, but, more importantly, makes Van aware that she has abandoned all hope that he will ever marry her. In this act of double renunciation, Nanda, for the first time, expresses a pure, selfless love; selfless because she has come to see Van not as a self-reflecting image, but as a man whose identity changes with the flow of time, a man who, like herself, loves an ideal of innocence that he knows to be impossible.

The bitter knowledge that brings Nanda to this full consciousness and allows her to view both Van and herself as flawed, mutable human beings is her recognition of "the law of change"—a law from which she had once declared herself exempt. "Of course I know everything changes," she tells Van in their final interview, "It's the law—what is it?—'the great law' of something or other. All sorts of things happen—things come to an end" (p. 506). In a discussion with Mitchy immediately afterward, she recognizes that she has been changing from the moment of her birth: "there was never a time when I didn't know *something* or other, and . . . I became more and more aware, as I grew older, of a hundred little chinks of daylight" (p. 528). Nanda's recognition of the impermanence of her own identity is the inevitable result of her perception of the changes in those around her: marriage has reduced the gay, rambunctious Mitchy to a quiet cuckold; little Aggie has ceased to frolic in the nursery and begun new games in the boudoir; Mrs. Brook's social circle is "falling to pieces." "The spell's broken," she laments, "the harp has lost its string. We're not the same thing." By the end of the novel, Van too has undergone a significant metamorphosis. The beauty of Nanda's renunciation has made him ashamed of his inability to love her and, perhaps, of his cherished ideal of innocence. After the incident at Tishy Grendon's, he ceases to visit Buckingham Crescent, returning only to bid Nanda a final farewell. When he arrives, Nanda discovers that the once self-assured and imperturbable gentleman has become nervous, awkward, and tongue-tied in her presence. Recalling the Van she used to know, she is quick to realize the irony of "having changed places with him"—it is now she who comforts and advises, she who urges Van to return to the society of her mother.

Although Nanda is eager to send Van back into life's whirlpool of sensations, she remains unwilling to submit to it herself. No sooner does she come to a full recognition of temporal reality than she retreats from it. She conducts her final interviews, not in her mother's drawing room, but in a special chamber upstairs where she has sequestered herself since Longdon's abrupt departure months before, a chamber lined with books that Longdon has sent to her, "nick-nacks," and "numerous photographed friends" (p. 491). No longer able to believe in the integrity of her own identity or the permanence of those around her, Nanda, like Longdon, has retreated into a cloistered world of static images. Her room, however, is only a kind of antechamber to a more perfect habitation—Longdon's museum world. Like the telegraphist, Nanda has come to realize that it is finally impossible to define one's identity in relation to a living image, be it Van or little Aggie—only the dead are beyond change, and only in the worship of the dead does one achieve the illusion of permanence. Unable to accept the nightmare of temporal reality, the ceaseless weaving and unweaving of herself, Nanda arranges to return to Longdon's estate "for a long, long [time]" (p. 510). Although she realizes that neither she nor her host can ever again imagine her as Lady Julia, she hopes to establish her identity, as Longdon has done, in the service of an immortal image. To reverse Nanda's earlier phrase, "if Longdon has Lady Julia, so Nanda's got her too." Sharing in his adoration, she will become, as Leon Edel appropriately puts it, "a treasured virgin, a priestess at a bachelor's altar."[27]

It has long been a commonplace of criticism of *The Awkward Age* to view Nanda's decision to abandon her mother's society as an act of sublime renunciation, a moral triumph over a corrupt world. Nanda is, after all, James' heroine, and there is a natural temptation to assume that the novelist, who had fled London himself only a few years before, is speaking through her. What drives Nanda into retreat, however, is not her sense of moral outrage at discovering either Aggie's degradation or her mother's illicit passion for Van. She assures Mitchy that, despite her excesses, "Aggie's only trying to find out . . . what sort of a person she is" (p. 528), and goes so far as virtually to encourage Van to become her mother's lover. The corruption of innocence is not the underlying problem either for Nanda or her creator in *The Awkward Age*—it is simply a manifestation of the universal principle of change, out of which there arose for James the central problems of human experience: the chaos of identity and the isolation of the self. Innocence appeals to Nanda, not because it is moral, but because she associates it with a timeless state of being. Her flight at the end of the book is not from sexual corruption, but from temporal change. Yet Nanda reflects only one side of Henry James. While James acutely understood "the nightmare" of individual consciousness from which his heroine retreats, he knew also that to deny the free play of awareness through the worship of a dead image was to confine oneself to a living death. If James had enshrined the image of Minny Temple in his memory, he had also lived for over fifty years at the highest pitch of perceptual awareness. Even in his isolation, James knew that if man was ever to go beyond image-love, if he was ever to escape the self long enough to recognize the autonomy of another human being, he could do so only in the world of flux and sensory stimulation.

Three years after *The Awkward Age*, Lambert Strether—a fifty-five-year-old bachelor like Longdon—would sit in a Parisian garden and passionately advise a young friend to submit to this world, to "live . . . live all you can." There is no such cry of affirmation in 1899, however—only a voice that seems to grow more desperate in its questioning. Like Eliot's Celia in *The Cocktail Party*, James seems to ask:

> Can we only love
> Something created by our own imagination?
> Are we all in fact unloving and unlovable?
> Then one is alone, and if one is alone
> Then lover and beloved are equally unreal
> And the dreamer is no more real than his dreams.[28]

THE DISTURBED MIDNIGHT

At the end of *The Awkward Age*, James' sympathies seem to come to rest in a borderland of doubt—an uncharted territory somewhere between the tumultuous chaos of Buckingham Crescent and the ghastly stillness of Longdon's mansion. James does not explicitly choose between these worlds, but, in this stylistically most impersonal and "dramatic" of novels, he leaves us to ponder a final tableau of Nanda sobbing on the eve of her departure for Longdon's. When Longdon reminds her that she is still half in love with Van, "her buried face could only after a moment give way to the flood, and she sobbed in a passion as sharp and brief as the flurry of a wild thing for an instant uncaged . . ." (p. 540). Like the telegraphist, who buries herself in Mr. Mudge's "little home," Nanda sobs only once before entering a prison where she will lock up her passion forever.

Nanda and Longdon are not the first of James' characters to devote their lives to the worship of the dead. The love that his earliest invalid heroes bear for a pale, icy virgin in stories like "Osborne's Revenge," "A Most Extraordinary Case," and "Longstaff's Marriage" suggests a fatal attraction to the image of a corpse. Although this macabre element is, as I have noted, generally subordinate to a life impulse in James' fiction of the 1880s and early 1890s, a survey of the novels and tales written in the late 1890s reveals an almost necrophilic fetish. As early as 1895 in "The Altar of the Dead," we find a Jamesian protagonist spending his life in burning candles to a dead girl. Stransom meets and falls in love with a woman who shares his obsession, but dies at his altar in his moment of surrender to her. Like May Bartram of "The Beast in the Jungle," this unnamed worshiper could have rescued her lover from the morass of his morbid introspection, but Stransom's own love, like Marcher's, dawns too late. When his heart convulses with love, it breaks, and his face is spread with "the whiteness of death." Although the story was written on the brink of James' darkest years, we still find in it an implicit condemnation of dead-image worship at the expense of life. After the completion of *The*

Awkward Age, however, James' attitude toward this kind of love seems to vacillate ambiguously from work to work.

"The Tone of Time," a sardonic little tale composed during the winter of 1899-1900, reveals the perverse cruelty of a female painter, Miss Tredick, who brings her dead lover's image to life on canvas. Commissioned through a friend (James' narrator) to produce the portrait "of an imaginary husband" for the wealthy Mrs. Bridgenorth, she paints instead the countenance of the man who had jilted her long ago. Torn between love and hatred, Miss Tredick portrays a handsome, insufferably insolent man, only to discover that the subject of her picture had also been Mrs. Bridgenorth's lover and would have married her but for his sudden death. As in the early tale, "The Story of a Masterpiece," which may be seen as a prototype, artist and employer mutually discover that they have loved the same image. In "The Tone of Time," however, neither party is able to free herself from her obsession and, in loneliness, each aging lady struggles to take possession of the dead lover's memory. Mrs. Bridgenorth's desperate longing for the portrait only heightens the painter's terrible jealousy. Unlike Stransom, who learns to share his altar with another, and Longdon, who invites Nanda to join him in his devotion to Lady Julia, Miss Tredick must have the image all to herself. In steadfastly refusing to sell her remembered likeness at any price, she revenges herself upon the woman whom she believes to have stolen her lover. If, by the turn of the century, James could imagine a self-absorption so extreme that it sought not only to enshrine a dead image, but to guard it from the rest of the world, he could conceive of a still more curious situation is which not two, but three necrophiles blissfully worship the same image.

"Maud-Evelyn," written during the same winter as "The Tone of Time," is perhaps the most bizarre and perplexing tale in James' entire canon. In composing the story, James may have had in mind Browning's poem "Evelyn Hope," in which the speaker, lamenting the death of a young girl who scarcely knew him, cries to her, "I claim you still for my love's sake!"[29] James' protagonist, Marmaduke, may be said to act out psychologically the full implica-

tions of this claim. After being turned down in a marriage proposal, the young man falls "madly" in love with the photograph of a
dead adolescent girl whom he had never met. Maud-Evelyn's dot-
ing parents have never really accepted the death of their only
child, and, with their support, Marmaduke not only conjures up a
shared past with the girl, but also makes her grow up, woos her,
marries her, watches her die, and mourns her. Robbed of his reason for living, at this point, he peacefully dies himself. So innocu-
ous is his dementia, so contented is he in his fantasy love, and so
exemplary is his conduct that he arouses our wonder more than
our disapprobation. In a final, bizarre twist, James insinuates that,
after Marmaduke's death, the girl who had rejected him in marriage is about to adopt his fantasy world. The most remarkable im-
plication of the story is that, although living in the past normally
freezes time for the individual, the imagination can create process
as well as stasis, can generate its own fantastic present around a
dead image. In "Maud-Evelyn," James appears to have discovered
that the final reductio ad absurdum of human experience is not the
flux of perceived reality, but that of the conscious imagination. To
endow a figment of our own creation with life, even in the sphere
of our own fantasy, is ultimately to destroy the thing we love.

In Stransom, Longdon, Nanda, Miss Tredick, and, finally,
Marmaduke, James had explored slightly differing strategies for
bringing an image of the past into the present. As these strategies
become more and more desperate and improbable, they progressively anticipate the unfinished novel of the supernatural that was
to mark the end point of death worship in James' "disturbed midnight." In fictions like The Turn of the Screw, "The Great Good
Place," "Maud-Evelyn," and, preeminently, The Sacred Fount,
James records the fantasies of his individual characters, but The
Sense of the Past, begun early in 1900, is an all-inclusive fantasy
of James' own. The world of 1820 into which the protagonist retreats is neither a dream, nor an hallucination, nor an upwelling of
madness, nor simply an historical atmosphere—it is the actual past
itself, the palpable realm of the novel.

James' hero, Ralph Pendrel, of New York, feels lost amid the surging chaos of industrial America. Finding himself in a society that has almost no cultural tradition, and which seems to be plunging recklessly into an unknown future, the young historian spends his life attempting to recapture a European past that he has only read about. Like Proust's Marcel, Ralph longs to "recover the lost moment, to feel the stopped pulse . . . to be again consciously that creature that had been, to breathe as he had breathed and feel the pressure he had felt."[30] James' time traveler has neither the cathedral at Combray nor the Champs Élysées to feed his "sense of the past," but he is born with a clairvoyant intuition that he was once someone else. In longing "to remount the stream of time . . . to bathe in its upper more natural waters," Ralph hopes to anchor his identity in a world where events are historically predetermined, a world in which, with his consciousness of the present, he might view the entire pattern of his life in a single moment. "His interest was all in the spent and displaced, in what had been determined and composed round about him, what had been presented as a subject and a picture, by ceasing—so far as things ever cease—to bustle or even to be. It was when life was framed by death that the picture was really hung up" (p. 48). Ralph wishes to become a figure in this picture, and, again like Marcel, he senses that there are places in the physical universe that might serve as psychic gateways into the past, "particular places where things have happened, places enclosed and ordered and subject to the continuity of life mostly" (p. 34). Before Ralph finds the portrait "framed by death" through which he will enter another age, however, he is rejected in a marriage suit, as Marmaduke had been. The object of his futile devotion is a rich, young widow, Aurora Coyne, whom he imagines as resembling "some great portrait of the Renaissance." He sees her as "an Italian princess of the *cinque-cento*, and Titian or the grand Veronese might . . . have signed her image" (p. 7). The fiercely anti-European Aurora is, of course, no more like an Italian princess than the faded Serafina is like Theobald's imaginary madonna or Nanda is like her grandmother. Ralph's beloved is enamored of the American present and wants a man who embodies its dynamic, restless energy. "I like men of action," she tells him, "men who've been through something" (p. 11). In his dedication to history, Ralph has become "too intellectual"; he has sought adventure, neither on the frontier, nor in the jungle of American business, but only in the sphere of his imagination. When Aurora gently refuses his offer, he senses the impossibility of ever finding an unchanging old-world image in the present and is filled with "a sad sense of having staked his cast, after all, but on the sensibility of a painted picture" (p. 8).

Just prior to his rejection, Ralph had learned that a distant uncle has recently died, leaving him a large eighteenth-century house in London. This elderly kinsman's generosity was inspired by his reading of Ralph's book "An Essay in Aid of the Reading of History." Before Ralph can journey back in time, he must journey in space from America to England, where the very air seems suffused with the tangible past. Following Howells' "really inspired" suggestion that he write "an international ghost" story,[31] James ironically compares Ralph's journey into the unexplored domain of his own past to Columbus' voyage to the new world. While sailing toward England, Ralph "sniffed the elder world from afar very much as Columbus had caught on his immortal approach the spices of the Western Isles" (p. 58). A quarter of a century earlier, James' own Christopher Newman had made the same ocean crossing, but, in 1900, the "new world" lies through the gateway of the old. Ralph Pendrel is journeying not simply into another culture, nor simply into another time, but into the depths of his own psyche. The "new world" that James himself was on the threshold of exploring was, as we shall see, the uncharted territory of the human unconscious.

Ralph thinks of his trip to England as a kind of quest undertaken to prove to Aurora that he is a "man of action." He hopes to return again after a year and win her hand, but there is deeper love, some " 'other' passion . . . within the pale of romance" (p. 43), which drives him to the land of his ancestors. It is his intuitive longing for a past existence, a passion that reaches its ghostly climax when he visits the house that he has inherited. Crossing the threshold is like walking into another century, and Ralph returns night after night to examine the portraits and stroll through the time-hallowed halls. During these peregrinations, he is especially intrigued by the portrait of a distant relative, also named Ralph Pendrel, who is inscrutably represented with his back turned to the viewer, "for all the world as though he had turned within the picture." The young man is, of course, Ralph's past self, who, with his "sense of the future," is looking away into the present, just as Ralph has been gazing into the past. Determined to solve the portrait's mystery, Ralph returns one night to view it by candlelight and discovers that the young man has turned to reveal his face; the face is Ralph's own. By the pale glow of his taper, Ralph stares at his double with the fascination of Narcissus suddenly beholding his reflection in the water. Like Nanda, he has fallen in love with an image of himself, an "alternate friend" who has always hovered just beneath the surface of his consciousness and who has drawn him gradually to this moment of self-recognition. In returning to the world of 1820, Ralph fulfills the wild hope that Nanda could only dream about—he becomes the image he loves.

James abandoned his novel during the early months of 1900, after two and a half chapters, or shortly after Ralph's dramatic discovery of the living portrait. Although he picked the manuscript up again in June, he found that he could not go on with it. "I am laying it away on the shelf," he wrote to Howells, "for the sake of something that *is* in it."[32] On the shelf it stayed until 1914, when James undertook to finish it; but in the intervening years his conception of the "something that *is* in it" had become somewhat clearer. At the turn of the century, James' notes on *The Sense of the Past* indicate that, after abandoning "the serious, the sincere things"[33] that he could not "gouge out" in the 50,000-word limit set by his publisher, he had come to think of the novel mainly as a ghost story, whose "prime beauty" lay in "the fancy of the revealed effect of 'terror,' the fact that the young man had himself become a source of it."[34] Since Ralph would know the histories of the men and women he meets in the past, his knowledge would make him appear as a frightening voice of fate. The problem that James faced, however, was how to transport Ralph into the past. The idea of using an ancestral double as a link between past and present seems simple enough, but, in attempting to delineate the exact relationship between Ralph and his pictured image, his narrative ground to a stop. Upon taking up the novel fourteen years later, "with a fine, fine little silver thread of association serving to let it dangle in the chamber of the mind," James recalls that "the jump . . . to the far off time, from the present period to the 'Past,' involved in the title, was going to have to be somehow bridged. I don't think I quite saw the bridge; I was groping my way to it with difficulty. . . ."[35] The extensive notes in which James proceeds to reconstruct his original plan for the novel suggest, I think, that what he was "groping" toward in 1900 was nothing less than a new conception of human identity.

James' 1914 recollection indicates that the novel was originally undertaken in a spirit of profound psychological interest. The man in the portrait was intended to be not simply a historical double, as his earlier notes and the first two chapters of the book tend to suggest, but a psychic counterpart as well. The "tremendously engaged and interested hero is [the] *alter-ego* of a past generation of his race."[36] In fact, "the two young men [are] each the *alter-ego* of the other."[37] Ralph's transmigration into the world of 1820 was to be an excursion not simply into the past, but into his buried self. Each Ralph is the unconscious counterpart of the other, and their exchange of historical roles was to be not merely a substitution of identities, but "a conscious and understood fusion." In James' plan, the knife edge between the conscious and the unconscious was to dissolve, and each Ralph was to become both himself and part of the other, a "double consciousness."

In 1900, James had broken off his story in the middle of chapter three, as Ralph was laboring to explain his relationship to the portrait to an American ambassador.[38] Clearly, this was the point at which the novelist had to consider and clarify the full psychological implications of his doppelgänger technique. It was here that, through the detested process of "simplification," he might possibly preserve a ghost story at the expense of his more ambitious, but only partly defined, ideas. James voiced his frustration at this dilemma in a notebook entry of August, 1900: "I don't mind, God knows, the mere difficulty [of treating "difficult" and "complex" concepts], however damnable; but it's fatal to find one's self in for a subject one can't possibly treat, or hope, or begin, to treat, in the space . . . as the thing *has* to be but the 50,000, the important, the serious, the sincere things I have in my head are all too ample for it."[39] When, after minor revisions to the first two and a half chapters, James returned to his narrative in 1914, it was not, as Percy Lubbock has suggested, "to work upon a story of remote, phantasmal life,"[40] but to explore the psychologically "ample" things that he had once been forced to abandon. In lines that echo the 1914 notebook, Ralph explains to the ambassador that he and his double are part of the same psychic fabric: "The point is, that I'm not myself . . . I'm somebody else" (p. 97). Although the two have not "merged" identities, they are at "opposite poles" of the same unified being. Each contains a partial awareness of what the other consciously knows; that is, of the knowledge that lies in his own unconscious. Thus, when Ralph takes the place of his alter ego, he knows how to behave, not because his double has described the role he is to inherit, but through a kind of telepathic knowledge that has gradually risen to the level of conscious awareness. Moments after he has walked through the front door of his house and been swallowed up by the past, he recognizes his fiancée. Ralph immediately knows that he is "to make love, by every propriety, to Molly Midmore," because of a "foretaste as of something rare [that] had for days and days past hung about him like the scent of a flower persisting in life" (p. 121). What James had begun to sense in 1900, and understood more fully in 1914, was that to meet another upon some unconscious level, as Ralph meets his alter ego, would be to escape the prison of solipsism and get at a reality beneath the veil of our conscious impressions. When the ambassador refers to Ralph's alter ego as an "impression," Ralph admonishes him: "I see I'm an impression to you—and of course an extraordinary one; but he wasn't to me . . . in any such sense as that. . . . He was as substantial for me as I am—or as I *was*" (p. 102). In struggling at the turn of the century with a novel that he would never complete, James was nearing the threshold of an all-important discovery: if there existed in man some dark, unconscious other self, some dimension of being beyond the dome of ever-changing perception, one might find there the real "otherness" of another individual and so discover the boundaries of one's self. In what James, in his 1914 notes, called "my supreme denouement," the woman who had rejected Ralph in real life, "Aurora What's-her-name, under a tremendous 'psychic' anxiety and distress of her own, which has been growing in her commensurately with Ralph's own culmination of distress and anguish in *his* drama," makes telepathic contact with the time traveler and brings about his rescue from the past. Although James conceived this ending fourteen years after he had begun the novel, he was, as we shall shortly see, ready to grant such extraordinary powers to the unconscious in his fiction as early as 1902.

It is appropriate that James began *The Sense of the Past* in the first days of 1900, when the cycles of two centuries seemed momentarily to join, for, within his career, the novel fragment represents the union of two gyres of thought, two diametrically opposed visions of the self. During the 1890s, the world of James' novels and tales had become increasingly internalized until, in fictions like *In the Cage, What Maisie Knew*, and *The Turn of the Screw*, he presented nothing but the landscape of a single character's mind. In much of this fiction, we have seen that this world is constricted even further by the protagonist's tendency to focus upon a self-defining image within his sphere of awareness, to compress all experience into a single impression. This process of self-absorption reaches its end point when the world of one's perception becomes a mirror reflection of one's self; that is, when all experience is reduced to the worship of one's visible self-image. From this point of view, Ralph's fascination with his identical ancestor represents the purest expression of narcissism in James' canon. Indeed, when Ralph first sees his ghostly double across a candle-lit gallery, he takes him for his own reflection. As I have suggested, however, by the turn of the century, James had begun to realize that, when the psyche contracts to a certain point, the dome of consciousness shatters and we pass into another dimension of being. Ralph's discovery that the portrait is alive at the end of chapter two may almost be said to mark the exact point in James' fiction at which the meaning of "consciousness" suddenly begins to expand. "It was like the miracle prayed for in a church—the figure in the picture had turned; but from the moment it had done so this tremendous action, this descent, this advance, an advance, and as for recognition, upon his solitary self, had almost the effect at first of crushing recognition, in other words of crushing presumption, by their immeasurable weight" (p. 86). To retreat far enough into the "solitary self" was to discover a sphere in which one might escape that solitude. Like the Yeatsean gyre that is born out of the dead contraction of its predecessor, the expansive vision of personality that would inspire James' treatment of love and identity in *The Wings of the Dove* and *The Golden Bowl* arose out of the solipsism of an aborted novel fragment.

Before James could present a vision of love based upon subliminal communication, he had first to create another human mind with which the individual unconscious might interact. Ralph Pendrel discovers his own buried self, but, in *The Wings of the Dove* and *The Golden Bowl*, the unconscious minds of two separate individuals will simultaneously discover and merge with one another. If James was only partly convinced of the power of the unconscious in *The Sense of the Past*, however, his next novel suggests that he saw the fusion of two psyches as potentially more destructive than redemptive. After setting aside the unfinished ghost story, he turned almost immediately to a proposed 10,000-word short story in which he picked up the tangled skein of ideas involving the past and present, conscious and unconscious that he had just abandoned. Bound by no prescribed word limit, the novelist's imagination could dilate freely, and, by June of 1900, the tale had grown into a slim novel that has held readers in bewildered fascination for over three-quarters of a century—*The Sacred Fount*. The evergrowing group of critics who have explored the psychological labyrinth of the book might find a proper motto in one of the narrator's most frequently quoted lines: "*Voyons*, then. Light or darkness, my imagination rides me."[41] After reading the novel in 1901, Henry Adams claimed to recognize his own "insanity" in James: "the obsession of the idée fixe." Adams concluded that "Harry must soon take a vacation, with most of the rest of us, in a cheery asylum."[42] Rebecca West set the tone for much subsequent criticism of the book long ago when she wrote that "the small, mean story worries one like a rat nibbling at the wainscot,"[43] and Edmund Wilson later declared the novel "mystifying, even maddening." Since Wilson, nearly every critic of the work has noted that James' insistence upon telling an improbable story entirely from the point of view of an unnamed narrator casts "ambiguity" over the actual events and meaning of the story. No one, however, has yet commented upon the ambiguity that grows out of James' presentation of two differing views of identity in the novel.

The Sacred Fount is, on the one hand, James' most tortuous and extended examination of solipsism, or, as Dorothea Krook has called it, "the 'epistemological theme,' which turns upon the final incapacity of the enquiring mind to know with certainty whether what it 'sees' is fact or delusion."[44] James stations the reader within the cloistered skull of his narrator; we see only what he sees, and our vision shifts phantasmagorically as his shifts. An early critic described this viewpoint as giving the effect of peeping through a keyhole at a man peeping through a keyhole, and Leon Edel has more appropriately likened it to the subjective camera technique used in experimental films. What is essential is that the narrator has no intrinsic identity of his own; what we know of him at any given moment is simply the sum of his impressions. James does not even identify his protagonist with the label of a fixed angle of vision, as he does with "the telegraphist." During the course of a day, the speaker rambles from one vantage point to another, even as the world of his impressions continually spins around him. While the narrator's impressions constitute the visible world of *The Sacred Fount*, there is another unseen dimension of being and another conception of personality implied in his theory of human relationships. The idea of love as a force that drains and finally destroys the individual was implicit in many of

James' earliest tales. As we have seen, however, in stories like "A Most Extraordinary Case," "The Last of the Valerii," and "Longstaff's Marriage," what appears to be vampirism is actually a self-destructive impulse within the hero himself. It is his own impossible unrequited love that eviscerates him, not the active love of another. According to the narrator of *The Sacred Fount*, however, love becomes destructive only when it is shared by two people at the deepest level of being, only when it becomes a fusion of two unconscious minds.

Although James' original notes for the story in 1894 make no mention of this unconscious element, they suggest the process through which he would arrive at it six years later.

> The notion of [a] young man who marries an older woman and who has the effect on her of making her younger and still younger, while he himself becomes her age. When he reaches the age *she* was (on their marriage), she has gone back to the age that *he* was.—Mightn't this be altered (perhaps) to the idea of cleverness and stupidity? A clever woman marries a deadly dull man, and loses and loses her wit as he shows more and more . . . The two things—the two elements—beauty and 'mind,' might be correspondingly, concomitantly exhibited as in the history of two related couples—with the opposition, in each case, that would help the thing to be dramatic.[45]

It is hardly surprising that James chose to begin this tale immediately after dropping *The Sense of the Past*, for, as in the ghost story, his plan calls for a shift from a historical or temporal relationship to a psychic relationship. In this case, however, James would split Ralph and his alter ego into two pairs of lovers. Temporally, just as Ralph retreats into the past, the middle-aged Mrs. Brissenden appears to regress in time by growing younger and more attractive; and, just as the alter ego advances into the future in exact correspondence with Ralph's retreat, "poor Briss" acquires the stoop and wrinkles of advancing age as his wife grows proportionately more youthful. Psychically, just as Ralph absorbs the knowledge of his unconscious double, so Gilbert Long, the narrator hypothesizes, has drained the intelligence, wit, and energy from his lover, May Server. Meeting Long on a train platform, where both are waiting to travel to a weekend party in the country, the narrator is amazed to discover that the once boorish "heavy Adonis" has suddenly begun to sparkle with elegance and subtlety. When the narrator sees Mrs. Briss moments later, he senses that both she and Long have somehow arrived at their improved conditions at the expense of another. This hypothesis seems partly confirmed when, after his arrival, he finds that Mr. Brissenden has taken on the withered appearance of a sixty-year-old. With the help of Mrs. Briss, who seems unaware that she is draining youth from her husband, and the painter, Ford Obert, the narrator undertakes to find the missing figure in his equation—a woman who seems intellectually depleted. After an exhaustive search, he finally decides upon May Server, who, in the course of a conversation, reminds him "of a sponge wrung dry and with fine pores agape. Voided and scraped of everything, her shell merely crushable" (p. 101).

The narrator's theory of love finds its most appropriate image in the vampire kiss, which he calls "the deepest of all truths." One lover "gives the lips, the other gives the cheek" (p. 66). In the narrator's mind, however, this "giving" involves nothing less than the transference of psychic energy through the fusion of two unconscious minds. He reasons that, when, in "an intensity of relation," "people were so deeply in love they rubbed off on one another . . . a great pressure of soul to soul usually left on either side a sufficient show of tell-tale traces" (p. 26). The miraculous flow of intelligence from one mind to another could only occur on some level beyond conscious awareness, for, as the narrator marvels, Gilbert Long seems unaware that his mind is improving. The narrator believes that it is "the power not one's self, in the given instance, that made for passion," and that this "power" is "at best the mystery of mysteries." Through this mysterious agency, Gilbert Long has drunk so deeply from the sacred fount of May Server's mind that the narrator senses that it is her soul that speaks through him: "He faced me with another light than his own, spoke with another sound, thought with another ease and understood with another ear" (p. 118). In the white hot intensity of their passion, the lovers have become fused into a kind of circuit—unfortunately for May Server, the energy seems to flow in only one direction.

It has been a common tendency among critics of *The Sacred Fount* to view the narrator either as a surrogate for the author, who is probing the relation between art and life through him, or as a parody of the artist gone mad, or, as Wilson Follett has suggested, of Henry James himself. If we seriously examine the theoretical content of what the narrator believes, however—as opposed to the psychological method whereby he arrives at his belief—and, if we consider his theory in the light of James' developing interest in the unconscious, it seems reasonable to suppose that James was using his speaker as a vehicle for testing his own conceptions. Taken at face value, the narrator's theory seems preposterous, but, read as a kind of psychological allegory, his tale reveals striking and disturbing truths about human nature. Although love relationships do not cause people to age and grow younger as the Brissendens do, they often involve psychological dependencies and emotional demands that can debilitate and even destroy. We find aspects of the narrator's theory embodied in such "realistic" fictions as Stendhal's *Le Rouge et le Noir*, where one lover grows stronger as the other wanes, in Fitzgerald's *Tender is the Night*, where a doctor derives strength and creativity from his wife's mental illness and fades into obscurity when she recovers, and in Lawrence's *Sons and Lovers*, where Paul Morel becomes emotionally independent only after the death of his possessive mother. In 1900, James was not yet sufficiently confident to embody his expanded conception of "consciousness" in a novel of social realism. In *The Sense of the Past*, he had couched his still unsettled ideas in the fantastic atmosphere of a ghost story, and, in *The Sacred Fount*, he transferred this atmosphere to a man's mind.

The narrator's quest to find "a law . . . governing the delicate phenomena" of love relationships is essentially James' own search

for a psychological principle through which man might escape the
chaotic sphere of his own consciousness. If the narrator is obsessed
with his theory, if he is, as Mrs. Briss claims, "crazy," it is,
perhaps, a measure of James' own desperate need to find a source
of identity in a world of ever-shifting illusions. Indeed, the central
question of "illusion and reality" in the novel was, for James, really a question of identity. Both issues are resolved into a little
scene in front of a glass-covered pastel. The painting shows a man
"without eyebrows, like . . . some whitened old-world clown,"
and with a pale, lean, livid face. The man holds an art work in his
hand that, upon closer examination, appears to be "the representation of a human face, modelled and coloured, in wax, in enamelled
metal, in some substance not human. The object thus appears a
complete mask, such as might have been fantastically fitted and
worn" (pp. 50-51). Each viewer interprets the mask differently
from his subjective vantage point. When an onlooker suggests that
the harlequin is holding the "Mask of Death," the narrator coun-
ters that it is "the Mask of Life . . . blooming and beautiful," while
May Server sees it wearing "an awful grimace." If the painting is
meant to suggest the relativity of all conscious perception, it represents also the mystery of identity that the condition of absolute
subjectivity creates. Although the viewers may debate the meaning of the mask that the clown holds, his "whitened old-world
face" is itself a mask. The painter has piled illusion upon illusion,
and no amount of intellectual speculation will ever determine who
the disguised figure really is. Just as the clown looks out of the
painting from behind a protective pane of glass, the individual
viewer stares in from behind the circumambient dome of his
changing consciousness. The narrator wisely remarks that "It's
the picture, of all pictures, that most needs an interpreter," and
his desire "to know what it means" implies a desire to strip away
the clown mask and discover the real face beneath. For James and
his narrator, discovering the true meaning of the picture is analo-
gous to discovering the true nature of identity; both processes require going beneath the visible surface of personality.

For all its morbidity, the narrator's predatory theory of love

suggests a possible escape from the "solitary self." What transforms love into vampirism is not the idea of unconscious union,
but the fact that individuals do not have an equal capacity to love.
As Mrs. Briss correctly observes, "Whenever two persons are so
much mixed up . . . one of them always gets more out of it than
the other" (p. 66). One lover must always "give the lip," while
the other "gives the cheek." The theory is based upon a premise
that James would develop more fully in *The Wings of the Dove*
and *The Golden Bowl*; namely, that one's ability to express love,
to give fully of oneself, is proportionate to one's intelligence and
natural sensitivity. May Server, whose very name reflects her role
as a selfless giver, seems the most tragic figure in the novel because, like the great heroines who follow her—Milly Theale,
Maggie Verver, and May Bartram—her spiritual refinement con-
demns her to love more intensely than she can ever be loved, to
sacrifice much more of her own soul than she can ever receive in
return. James surely shares his narrator's tender sympathy for
May, who, "in her . . . exquisite weakness," flits pathetically from
man to man in an attempt to disguise her suffering and to protect
the man who has drained her. The novelist realized that, unless
people like May could find an equally sensitive counterpart in love,
the passion that liberated the mind from solipsism would be a
self-annihilating passion. Instead of defining the boundaries of individual consciousness, such a love threatened to destroy the consciousness of the lover altogether.

The overwhelming ambiguity of *The Sacred Fount*, the narrator's final inability to convince either Mrs. Briss or Obert or the
reader of his hypothesis, is a reflection, perhaps, of James' uncertainty about the psychological and moral validity of the conception
of love that the novel advances. The narrator's elaborately
wrought theory of love as a psychic fusion that destroys the soul
that nourishes appears to collapse like a house of cards when Mrs.
Briss flatly denies that either Gilbert Long or May Server has ap-
preciably changed. She says that Long is really as "dull" as ever,
and claims to have proof (from Briss) that the woman in his life is
actually the unaltered Lady John. As for May, far from seeing her

as a tragic victim of selfless love, Mrs. Briss accuses her of trying to make love to her husband. Although the indomitable lady may destroy the logical underpinning of the narrator's argument, she cannot shake his faith in its ultimate truth. James' speaker ends his bizarre chronicle by defiantly asserting that his adversary has triumphed, not through reason, but through rhetoric. He insists that "it wasn't really that I hadn't three times her method. What I too fatally lacked was her tone" (p. 219). James too, as his subsequent novels illustrate, fiercely refused to relinquish his hope that, through love, man might transcend the isolation of consciousness. Just as the narrator concludes at the end of the novel that he must submit his theory to "that prompt test of escape to other air," James, after immersing himself in the claustrophobic, phantasmal world of *The Sacred Fount*, resolved to test his vision of love in a more spacious realm, in "the altogether human order."[46] This "human order" to which James would shortly return is the multilayered social world of his three greatest novels—*The Ambassadors, The Wings of the Dove*, and *The Golden Bowl*—and his re-entry into this world, after almost a decade, decisively marks the end of his disturbed midnight.

FIVE

A Practical Fusion: *The Wings of the Dove*

All beings have two sorts of existence: one for themselves and one for the eyes of others. They are, and also they are to be seen, soul and image. . . . We must not stop at the effect on our eyes and senses. For what affects us is impression, not reality; we must go behind it to reach the knowledge to which every phenomenon can lay claim, for it is more than phenomenon, and one must find the being, the soul behind it.
THOMAS MANN, The Transposed Heads

BY THE turn of the century, James had discovered that, through an unconscious "power not oneself," the individual might escape solipsism, but he had initially presented this escape as something terrifying or destructive. Ralph Pendrel confronts his subconscious self in a haunted house by the eerie light of a flickering candle, and the subliminal union of May Server and Gilbert Long in *The Sacred Fount* destroys one consciousness at the expense of another. From the beginning, James approached the unconscious half of human identity in much the same spirit as John Marcher anticipates the Beast in the Jungle—with a strange mixture of hope and dread. His hope arose from an intellectual understanding that man's only liberation from the chaos of isolated individual awareness was through unconscious contact with another; his dread sprang, in large measure, from an almost hereditary sense of unfathomable evil lurking within the human mind. James almost certainly was aware that both his father and his brother William had been psychologically crippled through mysterious encounters with a terrifying "presence," a nameless specter that seemed to issue with devastating suddenness from some dark corner of their psyche.[1]

After a family dinner in May of 1844, the elder Henry James inexplicably sensed that a deathly spirit had stalked from his mind into the house and was "raying out from his fetid personality influences fatal to life." Within ten seconds, James' father found himself "reduced from a state of firm, vigorous, joyful manhood to one of almost helpless infancy."[2] After a long period of convalescence, during which he discovered the philosophy of Swedenborg, he came to view his shattering confrontation as a divine revelation, a purgative stage in the regenerative process of the soul. Long after his father's experience, near the end of his life, Henry James was to create his own self-haunted hallucination in the story "The Jolly Corner," but William was to suffer through an experience remarkably similar to his father's in life. Entering his dressing room one evening, William was suddenly stricken with a horrible fear of his own existence. He recalls that "simultaneously there arose in my mind the image of an epileptic patient whom I had seen in the asylum, a black-haired youth with greenish skin, entirely idiotic, who used to sit all day on one of the benches, or rather shelves against the wall, with his knees drawn up against his chin, and a coarse grey undershirt, which was his only garment, drawn over them enclosing his entire figure." Like his father, William felt menaced by a mysterious alternate self: "This image and my fear entered into a species of combination with each other. *That shape am I,* I felt, potentially. Nothing that I possess can defend me against that fate, if the hour for it should strike for me as it has struck for him."[3] After his ordeal, William rose from his own ashes not only as a religious philosopher like his father, but as a psychologist as well, and set the experience down in the 1901 Gifford lectures that were to become *The Varieties of Religious Experience.* William was far from denying the existence of a spiritual world beyond the human, but he believed that mystical experiences were inextricably related to the unconscious powers of the mind. In his penultimate lecture, he observed that, taking all manifestations of "religious mysticism" into account,

. . . we cannot, I think, avoid the conclusion that in religion we have a department of human nature with unusually close relations to the transmarginal or subliminal region. If the word "subliminal" is offensive to any of you, as smelling too much of psychical research or other aberrations, call it by any name you please, to distinguish it from the level of full sunlit consciousness. Call this latter the A-region of personality, if you care to, and call the other the B-region.[4]

At almost the exact time that William was explaining his own and others' religious experiences in terms of a "subconscious personality," Henry was exploring the power of that personality in his novels. Although William recognized, in his lecture on "The Divided Self," that "blasphemous obsessions, ascribed invariably to the direct agency of Satan" were actually "connect[ed] with the life of the subconscious self,"[5] he believed that this "subliminal region" of personality could produce mystically beneficial and beautiful experiences as well. From the vast unconscious "B-region" of the mind, there arose both "our delusions, fixed ideas, and hysterical accidents," and our "telepathic" insights, "supranormal cognitions," and religious ecstasies.[6] In the years just after 1900, Henry James seems to have come to a conclusion similar to his brother's. In *The Sacred Fount*, he had revealed his belief in man's unconscious capacity for predatory destruction, delusion, and obsession; in *The Wings of the Dove*, he considers the unconscious as a potential source of telepathic communication and as a means to discovering personal identity. While William was arguing that an individual might arrive at clairvoyant knowledge when inflamed with religious devotion, Henry was creating characters who achieve a supernatural awareness of one another through romantic love. So inextricably are human relationships interfused with the unconscious in the fiction of James' major phase that telepathic sensitivity becomes the index to one's ability to love. James imagined that to love at the highest pitch of emotional intensity would be to pass out of one's solitary conscious self and to discover the boundaries of one's total being through subliminal communion with another person. The novelist realized, however, that, if love were to nourish rather than destroy, the unconscious energy from which it drew life had to be shared equally between the lovers.

In *The Sacred Fount*, James had examined the nightmarish possibilities of a fusion between two unequal souls: the love of May Server and Gilbert Long is not a free, balanced exchange of psychic impulses, but simply the absorption of one consciousness by another. May's spiritual wealth, her unconscious sensitivity, compels her to love far more intensely than Long, to sacrifice much more of her vital consciousness than she can ever gain in return. Although James did not attempt to embody this concept of love as subconscious union in his fiction until 1900, he had considered the problem of imbalanced psychic sympathy in his journal as early as 1895. In the extensive notes for a short story that he never wrote, he ponders the fictional possibilities of a brother and sister who "see with the same sensibilities and the same imagination, vibrate with the same nerves, suffer with the same suffering: have, in a word, exactly, identically the same experience in life. Two lives, two beings, and *one* experience."[7] As in *The Sacred Fount*, this oneness is brought about entirely by the female's extraordinary sensitivity; the male lives in the external world and the female lives through him. "The brother suffers, has the experience and the effect of the experience, is carried along by fate," while the sister "understands, perceives, shares with every pulse of her being. He has to tell her nothing—she *knows*: it's identity of sensation, of vibration. It's, for *her*, the Pain of Sympathy."[8] In his notebook, as in his novel, James could envision only a tragic end to such a relationship—"a kind of resigned, inevitable, disenchanted double suicide." When the active male constituent "chucks up the game" of life in despair, "the other, from a complete understanding of the sensibilities engaged," kills herself in turn. In sacrificing her life upon the altar of her devotion, the sister, like May Server, was to be an innocent victim of her own beautifully refined consciousness.

We find James' final portrayal of this idea in the exquisitely poignant "The Beast in the Jungle," completed in 1903. May Bartram, one of his first truly clairvoyant heroines, spends most of her adult life viewing the world contentedly through the eyes of the man she loves, John Marcher. Marcher is haunted by a lifelong belief that he is destined for some sudden devastating experience, that he is "being kept for something rare and strange." As he grows older, his dread of this experience gives way to a greater dread that he may have missed it—he longs for the beast to spring. Understanding Marcher far better than he understands himself, May knows what her friend cannot bear to acknowledge: that he has wasted his life in futile anticipation, that he is the one man of all men to whom nothing is to happen. She understands something else, however, that Marcher, in his egotism, had not suspected. She prophetically sees that Marcher's springing beast will be his devastating realization that he has been blind to the one person who might have given meaning to his life, that "his escape would have been to love her."[9] James leaves open the question of why May should love a man of such inferior imagination, but he makes it clear that she is devoted, not to an image, but to a human being whom she comprehends thoroughly.

Clearly, the major problem James faced in establishing a relationship based upon subliminal union was the intrinsic disequilibrium in unconscious sensitivity that he saw between men and women. Martha Banta, in her unusual book, *Henry James and the Occult*, notes that the novelist's artistic sense of a psychological difference between the sexes was almost identical with his brother's scientific theory on the subject: "In an article of 1897, 'What Psychical Research Has Accomplished,' William James made distinctions relevant to his brother's fiction when he drew the line between the two different types of mind involved in psychical research. There are the 'feminine-mystical' mind and its antagonist, the 'scientific-academic' mind."[10] Although William notes that "no one type of mind is given to discern the totality of truth," he argues that the "feminine-mystical" mind is more attuned to the pulse of real life, to the raw "facts" of experience.[11] How much Henry was influenced by his brother's hypothesis is difficult to determine, but he was almost certainly aware of it. William's belief in the superior psychic acuity of women was based largely upon his inveterate observations of Mrs. L. E. Piper, a renowned spiritual medium and telepathist of the late nineteenth century. In 1890, William compiled a record of his findings for the

Society of Psychical Research in London, and Henry, who was in England at the time, read the report in his brother's stead on October 31. The report describes Mrs. Piper's inexplicable ability not only to read the conscious thoughts of William and his wife, but to make accurate pronouncements as well about family matters of which they were unaware at the time. After repeated sittings, William reported in a letter that he was convinced that "Mrs. Piper has supernormal knowledge in her trances, but whether it comes from tapping the minds of living persons or from some common cosmic reservoir of memories, or from surviving spirits of the departed is a question impossible for me to answer just now to my own satisfaction."[12] In a spirit appropriate to his telepathic investigations, the grateful William wrote to Henry, "I will *think of you* on the 31st about 11:00 A.M. to make up the difference of longtitude," and hoped that the novelist's "devoted brotherly act" would be "the beginning of a new career, on your part, of psychic apostolicism."[13] Over a decade later, Henry fulfilled William's hope in his fiction, and his chief subjects were, like his brother's, female.

The choice was only natural, for James shows a marked preference for the "feminine-mystical" mind throughout his career. Women, he believed, were better able to fathom the mysteries of man's most important connection, "the great relation between men and women, the constant world renewal." In an essay written shortly after the turn of the century, he remarks that, among writers, "It is the ladies who have lately done most to remind us of man's relations with himself, that is with woman."[14] Only the mystical, unconscious bond of love could define an individual's identity, his "relation with himself," because only in love could man escape the all-absorbing chaos of his rational conscious mind. Although May Bartram, Kate Croy, and Milly Theale are James' first unmistakably telepathic heroines, we catch momentary flashes of a superior, intuitive power in women from the early stages of his fiction. When Fanny Assingham admonishes her earnest, but unimaginative, husband in *The Golden Bowl*, "You don't know—because you don't see,"[15] she is only echoing Angela Vivian's remark in the 1879 novel *Confidence*, "Men are so stupid; it's only women who have real discernment."[16]

When James' heroines are in love, this natural "discernment" is elevated to a state of mystical awareness. In his first major novel, *Roderick Hudson* (1875), Mary Garland recognizes Christina Light as a threat to her love the instant she sees her at Saint Peter's. She "knew by that infallible sixth sense of a woman who loves that this strange and beautiful girl had the power to injure her."[17] Olive Chancellor of *The Bostonians* (1886) is filled with "a sort of mystical foreboding" that Basil Ransom is about to steal her beloved Verena. Her knowledge of Basil's future interference seems conveyed to her "by the voices of the air." In *The Tragic Muse* (1890), after Julia Dallow has rushed into her fiancé's studio and found Miriam Rooth sitting for a portrait, she remarks: "I knew it—I knew everything; that's why I came. . . . It was a sort of second sight—what they call a brain-wave."[18] Fleda Vetch of *The Spoils of Poynton* "almost demonically sees and feels where others feel without seeing." Maisie Farange, who is destined to "understand . . . even at first, much more than any other little girl . . . ever understood before,"[19] arrives at knowledge through "divinations," and Maria Gostrey, with her "prophetic vision," seems to Strether "the nearest approach he had ever met to the priestess of the oracle."[20]

Perhaps the most striking example of feminine clairvoyance in James' work before the turn of the century occurs in *The Portrait of a Lady* when Isabel visits the dying Ralph. After her cousin has grown too weak to talk, Isabel assures him, "We needn't speak to understand each other," and, on the morning of his death "in the cold, faint dawn, she knew that a spirit was standing by her bed . . . it seemed to her for an instant that [Ralph] was standing there—a vague, hovering figure in the vagueness of the room."[21] Like all of James' heroines, Isabel derives her supernatural awareness from the intensity of her devotion. Although we may occasionally feel, in reading James' late novels, that, if his universe were populated only by women, verbal communication would be unnecessary, it is only love that gives his women their mysterious powers. Although we can say, with Martha Banta, that James believed women to be better lovers than men, we seldom, if ever, find in his works a super-conscious kinship between two women. Kate Croy, Milly Theale, Maggie Verver, and Charlotte Stant are psychic wonders only because they are deeply in love; without their male counterparts—even blind, self-absorbed men like Marcher—James' sublimely sensitive females would not exist.

James knew that, if love was to be man's salvation, if it was to free him from the "solitary self" without destroying consciousness altogether, it would have to be more than the penetration of one mind by another; it could be nothing less than an equal meeting of two souls, an interpenetration of separate centers of consciousness. This equality would be possible only if both lovers somehow shared elements of the mystical feminine sensibility. In attempting to define the nature of this sensibility, Naomi Lebowitz writes: "It is the masculine will that raises the status of relationship to a religious or romantic ritual, but it is the feminine sensibility that keeps the relationship alive by disturbing ritual, by submitting it to the tests of change."[22] As we have seen, the most common manifestation of romantic ritual in James' fiction is the transformation of another individual, living or dead, into an icon of religious adoration. Through the worship of an unchanging image, the lover attempts to give fixity and permanence to his identity—but it is not only James' males who love in this fashion. Isabel Archer, the telegraphist, and Nanda Brookenham all attempt to frame their beloved as a perfected image, and all suffer for their mistake. Thus, although Lebowitz seems correct in asserting that "the hope for life over death [in James' work] depends upon the feminine determination to break through the portrait of life and to create new circuits of relatedness," we must remember that James' most complex protagonists are never exclusively "masculine" or "feminine," but androgynous mixtures.

Lisa Appignanesi has usefully suggested that some of James' characters seem almost "to demand a Jungian division of male and female parts into 'animus' and 'anima.'"[23] The "anima," or feminine part of the self, is "inward, not easily recognizable"; it is the part of the psyche that Jung believed to be in communion with the unconscious. Although all arguments about sexual identity hang precariously upon individual assumptions as to what constitutes male and female characteristics, it is fair to say that characters like Ralph Touchett, Hyacinth Robinson, and, in particular, Lambert Strether seem to have something in common psychologically with James' great heroines. They are, in a word, more "sensitive" than most of the males of modern fiction, more spontaneous, more introspective, more receptive to change. The task that James faced in incorporating his ideal of mutual telepathic sympathy into a full-length novel was to create a man who was, at once, masculine enough to stimulate a woman's sympathetic love and feminine enough to return it with equal depth and intensity. What was needed was a sensitive but still unformed male mind. The act of loving could provide identity through relation only if the consciousness of both lovers was fluid, only if the lovers had not yet learned to see themselves fixed in arbitrary social-sexual roles.

Lambert Strether of *The Ambassadors* approaches the perfect condition of psychosexual androgyny more closely than any of James' earlier heroes. Strether himself realizes that he is the product of "a society of women . . . which was an odd situation for a man." Unlike the rigidly masculine Jim Pocock, whose social identity depends entirely upon external appearances, "his preference for light-grey clothes, for very white hats, for very big cigars and very little stories,"[24] Strether has almost no sense of a fixed, outer self-image. He explains to Maria Gostrey that "from the wreck of hopes and ambitions, the refuse heap of disappointments and failures," his name, borne on the cover of an American journal, represents his "one presentable little scrap of an identity."[25] Unfortunately for Strether, this "scrap" symbolizes his indissoluble tie to Mrs. Newsome, to whom he owes allegiance as an editor, a fiancé, and a Puritan envoy. For all his sympathetic perception and capacity for change, Strether's continual awareness of these relations and of the demands that they impose upon him prevents him from loving Madame de Vionnet with the unbridled intensity necessary for telepathic communion. As he explains to Bilham, the defining conditions of one's life—one's age, one's background, one's responsibilities—restrict the full expansion of consciousness and cast the inquiring mind back upon itself: "the affair of life . . . it's at the best, a tin mold, either fluted and embossed with ornamental excrescences, or else smooth and dreadfully plain, into which, a helpless jelly, one's consciousness is poured."[26] Each individual dwells within his own mold, within the unique bounds of his perception, and each mold, each conscious mind, is sealed off from every other. Only the mysterious warmth of shared love can melt the individual mold and bring two total consciousnesses into fusion with one another.

Despite his inspired devotion, Strether sees Madame de Vionnet only with a conscious, subjective eye—an eye that half perceives and half creates, that freezes another's being in an image rather than penetrating it. Happening upon Madame de Vionnet at Notre Dame cathedral in Book Seventh, Strether momentarily fails to recognize her. Instead, "she reminded our friend—since it was the way of nine-tenths of his current impressions to act as recalls of things imagined—of some fine, firm, concentrated heroine of an old story. . . ."[27] Ever painfully aware that he must soon leave Europe behind, Strether actually pauses, in moments of heightened sensation, to create memory images of Madame de Vionnet that he hopes will sustain him after their separation.[28] During their last interview, he self-consciously composes an enduring portrait, framed by the glass and gilt and parquet of her apartment. "He knew in advance he should look back on the perception actually sharpest with him as on the view of something old, old, old, the oldest thing he had ever personally touched; and he also knew, even while he took his companion in as the feature among features, memory and fancy couldn't help being enlisted for her."[29] Not surprisingly, before returning to America at the novel's end, Strether appears ready to renounce active life in the outer world (which Maria Gostrey offers him) for the sake of this remembered ideal. Like his middle-aged counterparts, Stransom and Longdon, he seems destined to lead a life of celibacy in worship of a recollected image. In Strether's case, however, the image is preserved, not by death, but by distance, and it is gilded by a European splendor that he will always remember.

In *The Wings of the Dove*, James removed the impediment of age from his hero and took care to assign to him no fixed values of any kind. Although we know that Merton Densher is young and handsome, he suggests no iconographic image like Kate, Milly, or Aunt Maud. James characteristically speaks of him in a riddle of contradictions. "The difficulty with Densher," he tells us, "was that he looked vague without looking weak—idle without looking empty."[30] His capacity for "becoming" is as elastic as any adult male's can be in James: "He suggested, above all . . . that wondrous state of youth in which the elements, the metals more or less precious, are so in fusion and fermentation that the question of the final stamp, the pressure that fixes the value, must wait for comparative coolness" (1:48-49). Densher's social identity is no less malleable than his inner self. We know only that he "was young for the House of Commons, he was loose for the Army. He was refined, as might have been said, for the City and, quite apart from the cut of his cloth, skeptical, it might have been felt, for the Church" (1:48). James endows his hero with a spontaneity of consciousness and a freedom of destiny that he had heretofore granted only to his American girls.

If Densher is temperamentally part female, however, it may be said that his lover, Kate Croy, is part male. Not only is her headlong aggressive energy masculine, but the very consistency as well of her role as "the handsome English girl" suggests that she holds what Naomi Lebowitz has called a "masculine-fixed" rather than a "feminine-fluid" conception of her social identity.[31] From the opening page of the novel, James continually describes her as tense, feverish, and erect. She paces throughout the book like a predatory "panther," and one of her first thoughts is "of the way she might still pull things round had she only been a man" (1:6). Together Kate and Densher form a perfect physical-psychical androgynous blend; their obsession with one another springs from a spontaneous, almost magnetic, attraction that James calls "the famous law of contraries" (1:50). Each instinctively perceives in the other the vital qualities that he or she lacks. In Kate, Densher senses an abundant "talent for life," direction, resolution, and outward form; in Densher, Kate discovers "all the high dim things . . . of the mind" (1:50), aesthetic speculation, plasticity of being. Kate desires to mold, and Densher desires to be molded.

Held together in psychic equilibrium, the lovers eventually come to see the world through, what James describes in his preface as, "a practical fusion of consciousness."[32] In order for Kate and Densher to become sensitized to the same vibrations, they need only see one another once. At their initial meeting, Kate realizes, "it wasn't . . . simply that their eyes had met; other conscious organs, faculties, feelers had met as well" (1:53). So powerful and dramatic is their mutual attraction that it seems each recognizes in the other a prototype that has been buried deep within the layers of their subconscious. Unlike the delusional love-images of the conscious mind, this love prototype exactly corresponds to a real, three-dimensional living person and carries with it an intrinsic understanding of another mind. The moment they see one another, Kate and Densher escape the chaotic solitude of single consciousness; they cease to look *out* at life from a single window of perception and begin to see *into* another window. Kate formulates the experience of their meeting in a metaphor that, while reminiscent of James' "house of fiction," considerably broadens the meaning of "vision": "She had observed a ladder against a garden-wall and had trusted herself so to climb it as to be able to see over into the probable garden on the other side. On reaching the top she had found herself face to face with a gentleman engaged in a like calculation at the same moment, and the two enquirers had remained confronted on their ladders" (1:53).

When they next chance to meet, six months later on a subway train, they again find themselves drawn to one another through unconscious affinities. Already, even across the crowded compartment, they begin to read one another's thoughts, to anticipate one another's behavior. "They looked . . . as if she had known he would be there and he had expected her to come in; so that, though in the conditions they could only exchange the greetings of movements, smiles, abstentions, it would have been quite in the key of these passages that they should have alighted for ease at the very next station" (1:54). So much are their thoughts alike, that verbally articulating them "for each other, for each other alone . . . only of course added to the taste" (1:65). So acute is Densher's sense of shared psychic experience with Kate that, without words, "he could catch in her, as she but too freely could in him, innumerable signs of it, the whole soft breath of consciousness meeting and promoting consciousness" (2:179). Thus, while walking in the park, they can "move by a common instinct" (1:95), and, even more remarkably, carry on a silent conversation across the dinner table at Mrs. Lowder's. In this latter scene, when their love is in full flower, Densher does not even formulate a question before, "as a result of something that, over the cloth, did hang between them," Kate "struck him as having quite answered" (2:44).

Just as the love of Densher and Kate broadens James' concept of "consciousness" to include unconscious powers, so too, it redefines his earlier notions of identity. Since love demands a recognition of another's total consciousness, and since consciousness is ever changing, any identity that love provides must be one whose limits remain somehow unfixed. In James' earlier works the idea of an "unfixed identity" would have seemed an oxymoron, but *The Wings of the Dove* suggests a possible reconciliation of these apparent contraries. In the early stages of Kate and Densher's relationship, the experience of passionate love expands individual identity even as it defines it. To recognize, in its completeness, a distinct center of consciousness outside of one's own is to become aware of the limits of one's *conscious* identity, but to penetrate that other mind on an unconscious level is to discover the fluid vastness of one's *total* being. Both these kinds of identity are implied in Kate's remark to Densher: "It's you who draw me out. I exist in you. Not in others" (2:62). Kate's love focuses all her thoughts, feelings, and desires in a single point of relation; it defines her, insofar as one's conscious being can be defined, over and over again during each fluid moment of sensation. Although the lovers' consciousnesses change with respect to the outside world through time, they are constantly being re-formed in the same relation to one another. In Densher, however, Kate finds another, larger unconscious self. Through a recognition of the always expanding nature of Densher's being, she expands too. Real love, for James, is two minds moving symbiotically through the changing contours of experience, growing and metamorphosing together, evolving through one another. Finally, with *The Wings of the Dove*, James' vision of love comes to embrace sexual as well as spiritual forms of intercourse. Although James does not, like Lawrence, make sexuality the source of subliminal understanding, he acknowledges that sexual desire is an indissoluble component of man's total being. Densher and Kate are not the first pair of lovers to sleep together during the course of a James novel (that distinction must go to Madame de Vionnet and Chad), but they are surely one of the most passionate pairs that he ever created. Those critics who contend that James was unable to instill sexual desire in his characters would do well to study the scene at St. Mark's Square in which Densher, gripping Kate's arm, demands that she come to his room.

James' treatment of love in *The Wings of the Dove* as an impulse arising from the subconscious anticipates the work of such twentieth-century figures as Jung, Mann, Yeats, and Lawrence. For each of these writers, love is a spontaneous, unconscious recognition of a psychic counterpart. William James reveals an early awareness of this phenomenon when he writes that "falling in love conforms frequently to . . . a latent process of unconscious preparation often preceding a sudden awakening to the fact that the mischief is irretrievably done."[33] Freud's theory of "object selection" also conforms to this general view of love: young men and women seek "a memory picture" and so fall in love with "persons who can revive in them the image of [their] mother [or] father."[34] Carl Jung terms this unconscious picture "the anima image," which represents, not an individual's parent, but the contrasexual part of one's psyche, an image of the opposite sex that one carries in both the personal and collective unconscious. Like James, Jung believed that the human psyche was bisexual, but he held that we only recognize the characteristics of our unconscious sexual half in dreams or in someone in our environment. A man's anima-image, or a woman's animus-image, is really a mental portrait of his or her buried alter ego; we tend to be attracted to members of the opposite sex who mirror the characteristics of our unconscious selves. For Jung, then, the phenomenon of love, particularly love at first sight, is really a matter of self-recognition.

In a general sense, *Tonio Kröger* and *The Magic Mountain* may be seen as fictional illustrations of this idea. For Mann, however, the fundamental dichotomy in the individual psyche is not between male and female components, but between two antithetical personality prototypes: one is dark, mystical, passionate, introverted, and aesthetic, the other, fair, scientific, extroverted, and social. Each individual longs for his subconsciously buried opposite. As a young boy, the shy, artistic Tonio Kröger is infatuated with Hans Hansen, his blond, bourgeois antitype. Years later, he suddenly recognizes Hans' image in a young girl and promptly falls in love with her: "He had seen her a thousand times; then one evening he saw her again; saw her in a certain light, talking with a friend in a certain saucy way, laughing and tossing her head. . . . That evening he carried away her picture in his eye; the thick blond plait, the longish, laughing blue eyes, the saddle of pale freckles across the nose."[35] Mann presents this unconscious attraction in reverse in *The Magic Mountain*, where the fair-haired rational Hans Castorp develops an uncontrollable fascination for a mysterious, passionate Russian woman, Clavdia Chauchat. Clavdia, Hans later realizes, bears an exact physical resemblance to a young boy whom he had loved as an adolescent.

We find in the poetry of Yeats still another variant upon James' conception of love as the conscious mind's sudden crystalline recognition of an unconscious ideal. Like Freud, Jung, and Mann, Yeats suggests that each lover bears a prototypic image of his beloved within him and seeks union with it in the external world.

Although Yeats believed that a person's love-image often corresponds to the "mask" that another wears, the mask is paradoxically the truest, most deeply seated part of one's identity—the ideal opposite self that the beloved is striving to be. Each lover, depending upon which of the twenty-eight phases he is in, seeks to achieve unity of identity—the realization of his true mask—through the love of a particular image. While Yeats' wheel represents entire personality types, each type is distinguished, in large part, by its distinctive love-image. Yeats, for example, felt fated to love Maud Gonne, who, for a man of phase seventeen, was the quintessence of feminine beauty, "a Helen, a Pallas Athena." The women of Maud's phase, by contrast, striving for a mask of passionate purity, would "give themselves to a beggar because he resembles a religious picture and be faithful all their lives."[36] With Jung and Mann, Yeats held that, although our love prototype corresponds to a real human being, it also represents an aspect of our subterranean self, part of an idealized alter ego that *we* most long to become.[37] For each of these writers, then, the love impulse is largely a narcissistic yearning for a part of ourselves that we see embodied in others.

It is here that James' vision of love in *The Wings of the Dove* must be sharply distinguished from that of these descendants. Although Kate and Densher are telepathically related, they love one another, not as self-reflections, but as distinct, separate individuals. They admire in each other qualities completely extraneous to themselves and so define themselves by psychic contrast. Only by subliminally discovering the otherness of another consciouness, only by encountering a reality beyond the all-enclosing dome of cognitive awareness, can James' characters ascertain the boundaries of their identity. Like many of the psychologists and novelists who followed him, James saw love as a quest for self-definition, but, for James, this discovery required a psychic orientation diametrically opposed to the one that Jung, Mann, and Yeats explore. Whereas these writers hold that we realize our total identity by recognizing in a lover personality traits that lie buried *inside* our psyches, James' late novels suggest that we discover who we are only when we recognize in our beloved a reality that lies *outside* ourself. For Jung, Mann, and Yeats, the beloved is like a mirror whose perceived reflection adds to our conception of self, but, for James, the beloved is like a flame whose flickering light gives shape to the dim void of consciousness by defining itself from the surrounding element.

In envisioning love as an escape from solipsism, James faced an inevitable conceptual paradox. The mystical psychic union that love inspired had somehow to separate, purify, and define the individual consciousnesses of the lovers. Fifteen years before D. H. Lawrence would speak of the communion of man and woman as "a pure duality of polarisation," Henry James wrestled with the apparent self-contradiction of separation through union in *The Wings of the Dove* and *The Golden Bowl*. More than any other writer of his generation, Lawrence approached love and its relation to individual identity in Jamesian terms—a fact that ought to alter our stereotyped notions of both writers. Lawrence, like James, believed that love alone could free man from the unboundaried prison of his conscious self by awakening the vital unconscious within him. No less than the author of *The Sacred Fount*, he understood the horror of a world in which "everything was tainted with myself, skies, trees, flowers, birds, water, people, houses, streets, vehicles, machines, nations, armies, war, peace-talking, work, recreation, governing, anarchy, it was all tainted with myself, I knew it all to start with because it was all myself."[38] To see with only the conscious eye, Lawrence believed, was to see a world of phantoms, and to love only with the conscious mind was to make love to oneself. "I was a lover," he writes in "New Heaven and Earth," "I kissed the woman I loved, and God of horror, I was kissing also myself."[39] Like Kate and Densher, Lawrence's characters experience real love through a sudden, overpowering recognition of a subconscious prototype—in an instant they discover and understand a personality that is, at once, psychically affined with and distinct from themselves. When for example, Gudrun first sees Gerald in *Women in Love*, she gleans the essence of his character from his strange "unconscious glitter."

> Gudrun lighted on him at once. There was something about him that magnetized her. . . . "His totem is the wolf," she repeated to herself. "His mother is an old, unbroken wolf." And then she experienced a keen paroxysm, a transport, as if she had made some incredible discovery known to nobody else on earth. A strange transport took possession of her, all her veins were in a paroxysm of violent sensation. . . . "Am I really singled out for him in some way, is there really some pale, gold arctic light that envelopes only us two?" she asked herself.[40]

Gerald is drawn to Gudrun by a similar magnetism when he watches her dancing at Breadalby. "The essence of that female, subterranean recklessness and mockery penetrated his blood. He could not forget Gudrun's lifted, offered, cleaving, reckless, yet withal mocking weight."[41]

Having brought his own lovers to a similar pitch of mutual awareness in *The Wings of the Dove*, James faced the tortuous problem that obsesses Lawrence in his best work. Both writers realized that the love that defines the individual by making him aware of a vital consciousness outside his own also fills him with a longing to merge with, to dissolve into, the soul of his beloved. Love awakens a flame of "otherness" simultaneously in the consciousness of both lovers, and these flames yearn to consume one another, to burn as one. Nearly all dualistic conceptions of love in Western literature before James and Lawrence glorify this self-destroying fusion. Cecil Lang has suggested that this ideal was first advanced in Plato's *Symposium* by Aristophanes, who maintains that men and women were originally fused as double-sexed, eight-limbed, single-spirited beings, and that the mutual attraction of love is a desire to return to this condition of oneness.[42] The courtly love tradition, which originated in twelfth-century Provence and which has distinctively shaped the contours of our love literature ever since, is ultimately founded upon a similar desire for eternal unification. Tracing this development in *Love in the Western World*, Denis de Rougemont notes that courtly love seeks to annihilate individual human identity altogether: "Amor—the supreme Eros—is the transport of the soul upward to ultimate union with light, something far beyond any love attainable in this life."[43] In the literature of James' own century, Shelley's *Prometheus Unbound*, the Brontë's *Wuthering Heights* and *Jane Eyre*, Whitman's *Song of Myself*, Swinburne's *Tristram of Lyonesse*, and Rossetti's "Severed Selves" all celebrate love as a mystical, self-dissolving coadunation. As Lawrence suggests in his essay on Whitman, "this merging, en masse, one identity, myself, monomania,"[44] while it seems to be the antithesis of solipsism, is no better, for it destroys one's integrity as an independent being. Although James was given neither to prophesying nor to direct statement, his last novels suggest an awareness of this problem no less acute than Lawrence's.

The eventual failure of love in *The Wings of the Dove* is a direct result of Kate and Densher's "practical fusion of consciousness." So absorbed are James' lovers in one another that they sever themselves from all other sources of potential relatedness in the universe. Like all feverishly passionate lovers, from Tristram and Isolde to Catherine and Heathcliff, they come to live almost exclusively in one another. The climax of their "common consciousness" is a mystical merging of minds so complete that the lovers cease to be aware of themselves as autonomous beings. This occurs when they perceive the world not merely through similar frames, but through a single frame of vision, when they see not only into each other's minds, but out through a single pair of eyes. Significantly, James makes this moment of Kate and Densher's most intense psychic union correspond exactly with the climax of the novel. When Milly descends in her white gown from the upper floors of the palace to "risk everything," Kate's eyes converge and focus with Densher's in a single moment of vision. "There before [Densher] was the fact of how Milly tonight impressed him, and his companion, with her eyes in his own and pursuing his impression to the depths of them, literally now perched on the fact in triumph. She turned her head to where their friend was again in range, and it made him turn his, so they watched a minute in concert" (2:229). Kate's "triumph" in this scene lies in the fact that, having revealed her plot in full to Densher moments earlier, she has made her lover see Milly through her own eyes for an instant. This moment of visionary unity seals their covenant in crime even more than their sexual union that follows. It is from this precise point in the novel that the destinies of Kate, Densher, and Milly are set on their sad, irrevocable course.

To say that Kate and Densher have created their own world, a world of single perception, is, in James' terms, to say that they have ironically approached a state of psychological alienation very like solipsism. When the lovers lose their sense of individual being, they also lose contact with the living continuum around them and so come to perceive the external world, human beings included, merely as a series of arrested pictures. In an essay written about the same time as *The Wings of the Dove*, James censures the Italian novelist Gabriele D'Annunzio for treating "love as a matter not to be mixed with life, in the larger sense of the word, at all—as a matter all of whose connections are dropped, a sort of secret game that can go on only if each of the partners has nothing to do, even on other terms, with anyone else."[45] James believed that, "from the moment [sexual love] depends on itself alone for its beauty it endangers extremely its distinction, so precarious at best. For what it represents, precisely, is it poetically interesting; it finds its extension and consummation only in the rest of life."[46] Passionate love, divorced from the larger circuit of relationship, "related, in its own turn, to nothing in the heaven above or the earth beneath," could sustain man neither in fiction nor in life. The failure of Kate and Densher's relationship lies in their inability, as psychically fused lovers, to recognize the consciousness of Milly Theale in its full complexity, to relate to her as a living, changing human being. Like every other character in the novel, they reduce James' heroine to an image, envisioning her as a totally innocent, unperceiving American heiress. No other character in James' fiction has inspired so many imaginative icons as Milly. To Kate she is "a dove," to Densher, "the little American girl"; Mrs. Stringham imagines her as a "princess" who has just stepped out of a romance, and Lord Mark sees her as the pale woman in the Bronzino portrait. James himself cannot resist depicting Milly variously as Christ looking vertiginously over the edge of a pinnacle at "the kingdoms of the earth," as a "pale princess, ostrich-plumed, black-robed, hung about with amulets, reminders, relics," who is confined to a tower surrounded by a black moat (2:139), and as "some noble young victim of the scaffold, in the French Revolution" (2:342).

In freezing Milly's vibrant character in a single image, Kate and Densher fatally distort reality and, as a consequence, falsify their shared consciousness. Out of love for Kate, Densher insists upon viewing Milly as simply a national type, against his deeper knowledge. This fixed image serves as a moral self-defense, for, by objectifying her as "the little American girl," he is able to imagine himself as standing in the same innocent relation to her as he had during their first meeting in New York. The moment he recognizes her as a rich, dying woman, desperately longing to live, and deeply in love with him, he is forced to conceive of himself as deceitful, mercenary, and cruel. Confronted with this frightening image of himself, Densher consciously suppresses his intuitive knowledge of Kate's true intentions, thereby blocking the channel of their telepathic communication and irreparably damaging their love. This love, which had begun as mutual expansion of being through a total openness to the flow of experience, atrophies, as all love must, when it seeks to permanently define itself in relation to a fixed image. It is ironic, then, that even in their most sublime moment of shared vision, when they see so deeply into one another, they should both see so little of Milly.

As Densher is gradually forced to realize his full complicity in Kate's scheme, his love for her begins to die. It is replaced by a new love for Milly, whom he has slowly come to recognize as a unique human being. More than any other character in the novel, Milly possesses a telepathic consciousness, a consciousness whose greatest discernments and self-deceptions are both inspired by love. Recognizing Densher's need to treat her as simply "the American girl," she conforms to that role but also willfully blinds herself to the real sources of his behavior. "They really as it went on *saw* each other at the game; she knowing he tried to keep her in tune with his conception, and he knowing she thus knew it" (2:255). As Dorothea Krook has observed, Milly is not the innocent American girl who is oblivious to her very innocence, but a mature woman who recognizes "the American girl" to be a role that she may choose to enact, but that she will always see beyond. Milly meets Densher only three times in her own country, but, like Kate, her attraction to him is spontaneous and overpowering. Her love is so potent and her understanding of Densher so deep that she immediately knows when he has returned to London. She arrives at this information through a sudden clairvoyant ability to see Kate through the eyes of Densher. On the night of her own scheduled departure from London, shortly after Densher's return, she looks at Kate and suddenly finds "that the image presented to her, the splendid young woman . . . was the peculiar property of some one else's vision. . . . Just so was how she looked to [Densher], just so was how Milly was held by her—held as by the strange sense of seeing through that distant person's eyes" (1:257). This epiphany lasts only fifty seconds, but it recurs a few moments later with even greater vividness.

Kate had remained in the window, very handsome and upright, the outer dark framing in a highly favourable way her summery simplicities and the lightnesses of her dress . . . she hovered there as with conscious eyes and some added advantage. Then indeed, with small delay [Milly] sufficiently saw. The conscious eyes, the added advantage were but those she had now always at command—those proper to the person Milly knew as known to Merton Densher. It was for several seconds again as if the *total* of her identity had been that of the person known to him—a determination having for result another sharpness of its own. Kate had positively but to be there just as she was to tell her he had come back (1:272).

The circuit of psychic interchange in Milly's vision is exceedingly complex. Milly's love for Densher allows her to see Kate through his eyes, and Densher, in turn, is able to see Kate's "total being" through his love for her. Thus, Milly can actually look fully into the minds of both Densher and Kate for an instant. It is this astonishing clarity of her vision that produces the "sharpness." Her discomfort is caused by a fleeting glimpse of the separated couple's full-blown love for one another.

Whereas Densher suppresses his deeper knowledge of Milly in order to soothe his conscience, Milly submerges her intuitive awareness of Kate's love for Densher beneath the surface of consciousness in order to nourish the dream that the rejected Densher may turn his love to her. This dream of love is so central to Milly's hope for recovery that it may be said that she deludes herself in order to go on living. She therefore allows her beloved to address her as an American girl in order that she may freely envision him as a wounded English suitor. Like the telegraphist, Milly knows that experience in the real world is likely to shatter her love-image, that the only way to preserve an illusion is to retreat into a static, private sanctuary. In ascending into the baroque upper chamber of her palace, Milly becomes the sable-clad, entowered princess of James' tableau. Although Densher obediently mounts to her chamber each day, like Rapunzel's prince, Milly understands inwardly that, if she is really to "live," she must surrender herself fully to Densher. This, she knows, requires a descent from her fairy-tale realm of air and sunlight and art into the lower Venetian world of canals and labyrinthine passageways, from the stasis of image-love into the flux of total emotional commitment. When Milly dons her white dress for the first time and leaves her chambers, she accepts life with full consciousness and asserts an identity that goes quite beyond that of a fairy princess or a little American girl or the Bronzino portrait. She is all of these, but indefinably more: "She was different, younger, fairer, with the colour of braided hair more than ever a not altogether lucky challenge to attention . . ." (2:214).

Although Milly's image of herself changes at this point, Densher does not understand the full dimensions of her character until after his final interview with her and his return to England. Her presence haunts him as Kate's ghost had seemed to haunt his chamber in Venice months before. On Christmas eve, as he is entering his apartment, he suddenly makes contact with her spirit and discovers the depth of his love for her. He sees many letters lying on his table, but his eyes "went straight to it, in an extraordinary way, from the door" (2:373). In a flash, he understands all that Milly has done for him, so that he can later tell Kate, "I recognized it, knew what it was, without touching it" (2:373). When he presents the letter to her unopened, she correctly observes, "You have your instinct. You don't need to read" (2:384). Densher's discovery of the letter corresponds almost exactly to the time of Milly's death (Mrs. Lowder receives a telegram announcing it late that night). It is as if, in a final triumphant act of consciousness just before death, Milly's transmigrating spirit united with that of her love.

Writing in a deeply meditative and personal vein seven years after *The Wings of the Dove*, in a little-known essay entitled "Is There a Life After Death?" (1910) James would inquire whether the very "quantity or quality of [one's] practice of consciousness"[47] might not ensure its continuation even after death. No "consciousness" in James' fiction is more sublimely spiritual, more deserving of immortality, than Milly's; and it seems clear that James had his heroine in mind when, at the end of the essay, he spoke of the human imagination's need to believe in its own eternal life: ". . . who shall say over what fields of experience, past or current, what immensities of perception and yearning, it shall not spread its wings?"[48] Yet, for all the passion and poetry of his inquiry, James lacked his brother's "will to believe" in the unseen and unknowable—he could go no further than ardent speculation. Thinking of his cousin, Minny, and perhaps also of William, whose death was still fresh in his mind, James pondered how any consciousness could "triumph" over the finality of death, "if *they*, wanting to triumph, haven't done it." For Densher, as for James, death remains an agonizing mystery. His telepathic communication from Milly on Christmas eve is the last he will ever know. After Kate has cast Milly's sealed letter into the fire, Densher thinks of it as "a revelation the loss of which was like the sight of a priceless pearl cast before his eyes . . . into the fathomless sea" (2:396). Bound to Kate no longer through a fusion of consciousness, but only by a sense of their shared guilt, he can scarcely bear the burden of his isolated awareness. After Milly's death, he envisions his relationship with Kate as an all-absorbing ocean, a "waste of waters," a "bottomless grey expanse," in which he is clinging to "a small emergent rock" (2:391). At times, he is filled with a need to escape his psychic isolation by plunging back into this sea of oneness; he feels that he and Kate must "bury in the dark blindness of each other's arms the knowledge of each other that they couldn't undo" (2:392). Like Lawrence, James had come to understand that the desire for blind fusion, for loss of self in another, was really a desire for death. What Densher ultimately desires, however, is eternal union, not with Kate, but with the dead Milly. Forced to endure life without her, Densher, like many of James' earlier protagonists, seeks the illusion of permanence in a kind of living death. In rejecting Milly's inheritance, he effectively rejects the ever-vibrant Kate and, at the close of the novel, seems destined to follow, rather perversely, in the footsteps of George Stransom, Longdon, Nanda Brookenham, and Marmaduke. Like these predecessors, Densher believes that the only source of stability in his life lies in the perpetual adoration of a dead image. Kate's parting remark, "We shall never again be as we were," springs from her painful realization that her fiancé has consecrated himself to Milly. "Her memory's your love," she tells him, "you *want* no other" (2:405). Densher makes no attempt to deny the charge. Like the pale woman whom Bronzino fixed eternally on canvas and crowned with a halo of golden hair, Milly will dwell in his mind almost as a religious icon—dead, yet hauntingly radiant.

Although James' hero reverts to a form of love that is hardly new, we leave *The Wings of the Dove* not simply with a sense of ruined possibility and wasted life, as in "The Altar of the Dead" and *The Awkward Age*, but impressed by the pathetic beauty of Densher's love. What distinguishes him from any other death worshiper in James' fiction is the novelist's intense sympathy. This affinity is partly explained by the fact that Densher's memory of Milly Theale is really James' memory of Minny Temple, who died of consumption when she was twenty-four. James had been traveling in Europe at the time of his cousin's death, and shortly afterward he wrote to William: "The more I think of her, the more perfectly satisfied I am to have translated her from this changing realm of fact to the steady realm of thought."[49] Although it is probable that James' love for Minny more closely resembled Ralph's platonic devotion to Isabel than Densher's romantic attraction to Milly, the intensity of his affection was extraordinary, for, over thirty years after her death, he was to immortalize her in his novel. Going one step beyond Densher, James enshrined Minny, not merely in memory, but in art. After the publication of *The Wings of the Dove*, he could write with satisfaction to an old friend that "Our noble and unique . . . little Minny's name is really now, in the most touching way, I think, silvered over and set apart."[50] Her image haunted James as being "so of the essence of tragedy" that a dozen years after the novel he could say that he had sought there "to lay the ghost by wrapping it . . . in the beauty and dignity of art."[51]

Notwithstanding James' intention, Milly Theale, whom he apotheosizes as a dove, an angel, a princess, and, finally, as Christ, is tragic only in the sense that the immaculate, victimized Desdemona is tragic in Othello. The greater suffering, as James surely realized in the final chapters of his novel, lies, not with the dead lover, but with the one who is condemned to go on living. The real tragedy of *The Wings of the Dove* is not the death of Milly Theale, but the death of the sublime, living love in which Milly, Densher, and Kate each share. Above all else, it was James' profound understanding of the extraordinary refinement of consciousness that this love demanded and of man's apparent inability to sustain it that inspired his compassion for Densher, who loses both Kate and Milly. In turning to image-love after Milly's death, Densher might be compared to one of the prisoners in Plato's cave, who, having glimpsed for a moment the "real" light outside, must return to a world of shadows. Densher discovers the real light of otherness in Kate and, fleetingly, in Milly, but the bitter paradox that James embodied in *The Wings of the Dove* is that the love that defines identity through communion with another consciousness eventually destroys it through the very intensity of that union.

In their separate fashions, James and Lawrence each rebelled against "the merging, the clutching, the mingling of love," and each understood that individual selfhood could be maintained only if both lovers remained in vital relation to other parts of the external world. For Lawrence, who believed that the same unconscious animating energy that bound man to woman was diffused throughout nature, the question of multiple relations posed less of a problem than for James. The concept of "star equilibrium" refers not simply to the identity that men and women discover through one another, but to their larger relation to rivers, oceans, mountains, and all the teeming, flowering life on earth. Through sexual love, Lawrence insisted, man and woman might be fulfilled in difference: "The man is pure man, the woman pure woman, they are perfectly polarised. But there is no longer any of the horrible merging, mingling, self-abnegation of love. There is only the pure duality of polarisation, each one free from the contamination of the other. In each, the individual is primal, sex is subordinate, but perfectly polarised."[52] This refinement of being is possible, however, only when the lovers discover their larger psychic connection with the sensory universe.

> Oh what a catastrophe, what a maiming of love when it was made a personal, merely personal feeling, taken away from the rising and the setting of the sun, and cut off from the magic connection of the solstice and the equinox! This is what

is the matter with us. We are bleeding at the roots, because
we are cut off from the earth and sun and stars, and love is a
grinning mockery, because, poor blossom, we plucked it from
its stem on the tree of Life, and expected it to keep on blooming in our civilized vase on the table.[53]

Just as the sexual love of an individual man and woman draws its
life from nature, so Lawrence believed that the underlying life impulse in nature itself springs from a primal attraction between
male and female. It follows that, for Lawrence, one's truest identity is as a purely crystallized male or female, and that, in discovering our sexual identity, we simultaneously discover our relation to
all the other male and female creatures that have ever lived. Thus,
Lawrence's lovers, having recognized the otherness of one
another, simultaneously establish a galaxy of other relations that
expand infinitely in space and time. Ursula can think of Birkin as
"one of the sons of God," because she understands that all other
males exist in him; Birkin imagines Ursula transfigured as "a
fresh, luminous flower glinting with golden light," because he
knows that she embodies all of the earth's fecund female vitality.

If Henry James' lovers fail to soar into this hypersensual empy-
rean, it is not because the novelist shied away from sexual passion,
but because he believed that psychic isolation was the natural condition of man. Lawrence could maintain that industrialized
societies turned men into solipsists, but James devoutly felt that
"loneliness" was "the deepest thing about one." The individual
viewers in his "house" of life are not connected by a living mem-
brane, but stare out of "holes in a dead wall, disconnected, perched
aloft."[54] Human love, at its most intense, might miraculously rescue the individual from his isolation, but there existed for James
no mystically animating, all-pervasive power in the universe. For
James, man was irredeemably severed from Lawrence's tree of life,
and, if love was to bloom, it had to do so in a "civilized vase on the
table." The unconscious that becomes clairvoyantly sensitized in
James' late novels is an aspect of the individual mind and streams
from no primal universal source such as Jung's "collective uncon-

scious," Yeats' "spiritus mundi," and Lawrence's "life flow." Two of his characters may generate a psychic circuit based upon unconscious affinities, but they can define themselves only in relation to hypersensitive *human* centers of consciousness. Each telepathic relationship in James' late novels is a kind of miracle unto itself. Unlike Lawrence, whose interest in the ever-proliferating structure of man's relationship to the universe diminishes the importance of the individual even as it defines him, James never submerges his characters in a mythic identity. For Lawrence, "it is the *relation itself* which is the quick and central clue to life, not the man, nor the woman, nor the children that result from the relationship as a contingency";[55] for James, the individual man and woman alone give meaning to love.

The obvious variance in James' and Lawrence's treatment of sex merely grows out of their radically different visions of man's place in the natural universe. While James held that sex must play a role in any mature love relationship—and it assuredly does in *The Wings of the Dove* and *The Golden Bowl*—he could never envision it as the fountainhead of self-discovery. Indeed, as we have seen, whereas Lawrence's best lovers are purely distilled males and females, James' are subtle, androgynous mixtures. Clearly, if James' lovers were ever to approach an equivalent to star equilibrium, it would have to be a polarization based upon something other than sexual identity. Real otherness required the discovery, not of a sexual opposite, but of another infinitely complex, multifaceted personality.

By the end of *The Wings of the Dove*, it is evident that no single relationship can sustain the sense of otherness upon which individual identity depends; to love another too intensely is to lose one's sense of self. Two lovers could remain poised in telepathic balance, acutely aware of each other's psychic boundaries, only if they each recognized the autonomy of a third consciousness. Since there can be no true recognition of another center of consciousness in James, save through love—particularly passionate love—it follows that the only way to maintain individual identity would be through the love of more than one person. Merton Densher loves

A PRACTICAL FUSION

twice in the course of *The Wings of the Dove*, but the heroine whom James was to create in his next novel, *The Golden Bowl*, struggles to define herself by loving two men simultaneously. Maggie Verver, the telepathically sensitive protagonist of this strangest and most bewildering of James' works, loves both her husband and her father.

SIX

For Love: *The Golden Bowl*
and *Final Tales*

Can Wisdom be kept in a silver rod,
Or love in a golden bowl?
WILLIAM BLAKE

THE plot of *The Golden Bowl* both recapitulates the love triangle in *The Wings of the Dove* and extends James' ideal of telepathic sympathy into the sphere of multipersonal love relationships. Once again, James framed his novel as an elaborately wrought scenario of passion and betrayal, employing the same basic formula that he had used a year before. A pair of young lovers, ardent and sensitive but, alas, impoverished, conduct an affair behind the back of an innocent American heiress to whom the young man has pledged himself. To enact this drama, James created a handsome prince of ancient lineage, a fair, fabulously wealthy princess from a distant land, and a beautiful dark-haired seductress who comes to the palace and casts a spell of enchantment upon the prince. So stated, James' plot transcends melodrama and, as Matthiessen, Krook, Lebowitz, and Appignanesi all note, suggests the "magical world" of fairy tales. Milly Theale had been a fairy-tale princess save for a title, and, in *The Golden Bowl*, James not only remedies this oversight, but converts the three-sided love story of the earlier novel into a four-sided one by providing his princess with an incalculably rich financial wizard of a father. Maggie Verver's love for her parent, as we shall see, goes beyond mere filial devotion and complicates the question of identity through relationship in the novel by placing her at the center of two love triangles. While Maggie struggles with Charlotte for possession of Prince Amerigo, she is also torn between her conflicting loves for the Prince and her father.

James uses fairy-tale devices to create a kind of symbolic framework in *The Golden Bowl*. And, in truth, the fairy tale serves as a perfect metaphor for the central psychological action of the novel—the quest for identity through love. The intensity of romantic love in the book creates circuits of telepathic divination that seem little short of magical. If myth is a record of the behavior patterns common to all men, fairy tales are, perhaps, a record of the fantasies that men have shared throughout the ages. As Lisa Appignanesi notes, myth dictates a behavioral structure that we recognize in real life, a structure that is fated by some transpersonal force, usually a god.[1] In fairy tales, however, characters exert a much greater control over their own destinies; human longing generates continual metamorphosis and magical transformations of identity—outcast children become princesses, frogs change into princes, mermaids into mortals, ugly ducklings into swans, cotton into gold, pumpkins into coaches. Significantly, these transformations are brought about by a mysterious power invested within either the central character or some humanized fairy godmother. Jung points out that, in fairy tales, as in dreams, the psyche (or protagonist) tells its own story, usually shaping and controlling the events around it.[2] Thus, while myths reflect man's interaction with the universe, fairy tales embody the relationship of the psyche to itself, often the relationship between our dominant self and the self that we long to be.

The heroes and heroines of our most popular fairy tales attain their identities as princes and princesses by overcoming a series of obstacles that separate them from their true love. Almost inevitably, it is the power of love that brings about the final magical transformation either of the protagonist's identity or of his beloved's, or both: Prince Charming awakens Sleeping Beauty with a kiss, a kindhearted princess kisses a frog and finds a husband, Beauty's declaration of love transforms the Beast into a man, a prince's enchantment converts a cinder girl into a princess, Siegfried's love for Odette breaks an evil magician's spell and changes a beautiful swan into a girl. In these fairy tales, as in James' final novels, romantic love is the source not only of transcendent power, but also of identity itself.

Although Milly Theale and Maggie Verver both conform to the role of the innocent little maiden who seeks the love of a prince, the fairy-tale structure of James' late novels suggests several different stories. A number of critics have observed that "the Cinderella theme"—of which there are over four hundred variants—runs through much of his work. Clearly, the story of a "little American girl" who comes to a foreign kingdom and, through the purity of her love, steals the prince from a dazzling but corrupted beauty is woven deeply into both *The Wings of the Dove* and *The Golden Bowl*. To read James' final novel simply in these terms, however, is to ignore the salient fact that it is Maggie who begins as a pampered "princess" and poor but beautiful Charlotte Stant who most resembles a cinder girl. This deliberate mixing of roles suggests that James was interested in a kind of psychic identity that could not be achieved simply by becoming a "princess." As we have seen, James believed that love could define identity only by freeing an individual from his condition of isolated self-consciousness, by creating in him a sense of otherness. In the legend of Rapunzel, James seems to have found a metaphor for the psychological isolation that his heroines must overcome through their love; the ivory tower becomes a potent symbol for alienated consciousness in his final pair of novels. Milly Theale is described as a black-robed "angular pale princess" sitting in a "tower," over which Kate Croy, "the upright, restless, slow-circling lady of the court" keeps watch "from the far side of the moat." Afraid to acknowledge her suspicions about Kate and Densher's love, Milly literally retreats into the upper floors of the Palazzo Leporelli where she imagines herself "remaining aloft in the divine dustless air." Maggie too, dwells in a palace, whose ancient walls shield her from the affair that Prince Amerigo and Charlotte conduct outside. In the "garden of her life," she naively thinks of the domestic felicity of her husband, father, and mother-in-law as "some strange tall tower of ivory, or perhaps rather some wonderful beautiful but outlandish pagoda, a structure plated with hard bright porcelain, coloured and figured and adorned at the overhanging eaves with silver bells that tinkled ever so charmingly when stirred by chance airs."[3] Later, after she has begun to suspect her husband's liaison with Charlotte, she imagines that the lovers have built around her "a vault [that] seemed more heavily to arch; so that she sat there in the solid chamber of her helplessness" (2:44).

The same transcendent love that allows Milly to descend from her palace and win Densher's heart enables Maggie to break out of her vault and reclaim her husband. In each case, the intensity of the heroine's devotion transforms her lover's perception, opens his eyes to the full measure of her being and, in so doing, creates in both of them a new sense of self. Love transforms perception, which transforms identity—and this is precisely what we find symbolically embodied at the end of "Rapunzel." According to the Brothers Grimm, after the wicked witch has cut Rapunzel's tresses and banished her to the desert, she blinds the prince with thorns as he attempts to scale the tower.

> Thus, the Prince wandered about in the forest quite blind, and lived on berries and roots, lamenting all the time the loss of his dear bride. For a year he wandered, and came at last to the desert where Rapunzel was living miserably. He heard a voice which struck him as familiar, and when he came near Rapunzel recognized him, and fell on his neck weeping. Two of her tears watered his eyes, and he recovered his sight and could see as well as ever. He took Rapunzel to his own country, where they were received with joyous acclamation. And they lived there many years, happy and content.[4]

In *The Wings of the Dove* and *The Golden Bowl*, as in Rapunzel, the heroine's love brings about a miracle of transformation that frees her from isolation and provides, momentarily at least, a new identity for both her and her lover. Unlike Rapunzel and her prince, however, the lovers in James' late novels—good and bad alike—do not live happily ever after. As we observed in *The Wings of the Dove*, and shall see in *The Golden Bowl*, the passion that defines individual identity eventually degenerates into a self-destroying fusion of consciousness.

Although James chose extramarital relationships to illustrate the breakdown of love in his final trio of novels, his couples fail, not because they behave immorally, but because of something in the nature of romantic love itself. Along with Strether, James had recognized the beauty of Madame de Vionnet's illicit love for Chad, and, in *The Golden Bowl*, he endows his adulterers with a greater vitality of passion and sensitivity to one another than any pair of lovers he ever created. Like Kate and Densher, Amerigo and Charlotte are bound together by a mysterious psychic magnetism—they spontaneously recognize in one another a love archetype whose consciousness is at once related to, and utterly unlike, their own. Once again, James implies that this affinity derives from a species of psychosexual androgyny in both lovers. Each sees in the other intrinsic qualities that he or she lacks. Amerigo, although he is outwardly handsome and virile, possesses a psychological inwardness and plasticity that is feminine. Like Densher, he is free of all constricting occupational male roles and has an almost infinite capacity for change. Fanny Assingham sees him as "younger than his years . . . beautiful, innocent, vague" (1:42), while Mr. Verver, delighted at his son-in-law's remarkable adaptability, speaks of him as "a pure and perfect crystal." "You're round, my boy," he tells him, "you're variously and inexhaustibly round, when you might, by all the chances, have been abominably square" (1:137-138). Passive, pampered, and equivocal by nature, the Prince initially senses no defining masculine identity even as a husband; he imagines wedlock with Maggie as an immersion in a "golden bath" and thinks of himself as "drifting" through "a thickness of white air" (1:22) like Poe's Gordon Pym.

Not surprisingly, Charlotte Stant is as outwardly masculine as Amerigo is inwardly feminine. At first glance, she is "a tall strong charming girl," whose face and form suggest "winds and waves and custom-houses . . . far countries and long journeys, the knowledge of how and where and the habit, founded on experience, of not being afraid" (1:45). Like Kate Croy, she exudes a male vigor and rigidity, a slim, sinuous strength that orients her toward social ritual and decisive action in the external world. She is the initiator in her affair with the Prince and the perpetual organizer of social activities at Portland Place and Eaton Square. Adam Verver compares her "practised passion" at the piano to one "playing lawn-tennis or endlessly and rhythmically waltzing" (1:202); Maggie describes her as "brave and bright"; and Amerigo thinks of her variously as "a huntress," a statue of silver or bronze, a "wonderful finished instrument . . . intently made for exhibition, for a prize," and, finally, a long "silk purse, well filled with gold pieces" (1:47). Like the golden bowl that comes to represent their love, the union of Charlotte and Amerigo suggests a fusion of hard outer metal and round inner crystal—a balanced mixture of masculine and feminine traits.

The moment Amerigo sees Charlotte enter Mrs. Assingham's drawing room, after years of separation, his former passion suddenly returns. "He saw her in her light: the immediate exclusive address . . . was like a lamp she was holding aloft for his benefit and for his pleasure. It showed him everything—above all her presence in the world, so closely, so irretrievably contemporaneous with his own: a sharp, sharp fact, sharper during these instants than any other at all, even than that of his marriage . . ." (1:45). Studying each facet of Charlotte's appearance—the shape of her eyes, the shade of her brown hair, the slight protrusion of her teeth—he finds that they conform to an image buried deeply in his unconscious. His sense of a shared intelligence with her spontaneously revives with his recognition of this image, as if through the agency of Proust's "involuntary memory."

> But it was, strangely, as a cluster of possessions of his own that these things in Charlotte Stant now affected him; items in a full list, items recognised, each of them, as if, for the long interval, they had been "stored"—wrapped up, numbered, put away in a cabinet. . . . While she faced Mrs. Assingham the door of the cabinet had opened of itself; he took the relics out one by one, and it was more and more each instant as if she were giving him time (1:46).

Charlotte's presence brings into Amerigo's conscious mind both his subconsciously remembered portrait of her and, from a still deeper depth, the original love prototype whom she resembles. We find clearer evidence of this underlying prototype suggested in a similar meeting later in the novel. When Charlotte visits Amerigo one rainy afternoon after her marriage, "the sense of the past revived for him . . . as it hadn't yet done" (1:298). Although the Prince feels an overpowering sense of déjà vu as he watches her drying her shoes by the fire, "he couldn't have told what particular links and gaps had at the end of a few minutes found themselves renewed and bridged; for he remembered no occasion in Rome from which the picture could have been so exactly copied. He remembered, that is, none of her coming to see him in the rain while a muddy four-wheeler waited and while, though having left her waterproof downstairs, she was yet invested with the odd eloquence—the positive picturesqueness, yes, given all the rest of the matter—of a dull dress and a black Bowdlerised hat . . ." (1:297). Amerigo seems to be responding here to a love-image that is deeper and more elemental than any specific memory, an image that must have existed in his mind even before memory and thought association began.

More than ever before, James' lovers appear destined for one another by an ineluctable power that goes beyond their rational understanding. Indeed, the complex network of conscious choices that gives rise to Charlotte's marriage to Adam Verver and, eventually, to her love affair with Amerigo, almost seems dictated by some combined effort of unconscious wills. Shortly after the marriage, Amerigo ponders how "Charlotte and he had by a single turn of the wrist of fate—'led up' to indeed, no doubt, by steps and stages that conscious computation had missed—been placed face to face in a freedom that extraordinarily partook of ideal perfection, since the magic web had spun itself without their toil, almost without their touch" (1:298). Only later, on the day when Charlotte and he consummate their love at Gloucester, does the Prince begin to realize that he has unconsciously helped to shape the conditions that make their assignation possible. Gazing at Charlotte, he suddenly "knew why he had from the first of his marriage tried with such patience for such conformity; he knew why he had given up so much and bored himself so much; he knew why he had at any rate gone in, on the basis of all forms, on the basis of his having in a manner sold himself, for a *situation nette*. It had all been just in order that his—well, what on earth should he call it but his freedom?—should at present be as perfect and rounded and lustrous as some huge precious pearl" (1:358). Henry James almost certainly did not know Freud's theories of the unconscious; yet Amerigo's thoughts reverberate with ideas like those of twentieth-century novelists who did. We are reminded, perhaps, of Lawrence's Birkin, who declares that all "accidents" result from unconscious desires, or of Hans Castorp, who, through his own unconscious effort, develops a tubercular lung so that he may remain at the asylum near the woman he loves. Although James' lovers do not, like Lawrence's and Mann's, speculate upon how their unconscious operates, they make greater use of the powers invested there than do most other characters in our fiction.

From the time of their first meeting, before the opening of the novel, Amerigo and Charlotte possess an extraordinary capacity for understanding one another. Charlotte's "almost mystifying instinct" for Italian and Amerigo's equally remarkable command of English suggest a pair of minds that are naturally attuned. After their separate marriages, this "associated sense" (1:346), this "perfect parity of imagination" is so stimulated by frequent contact that their communications soar above the spoken word. "You always make me feel everything," Charlotte marvels, "so that I know ten miles off how you feel" (1:359). Her remark is hardly an exaggeration: on the London afternoon when they renew their love affair, Charlotte arrives at Portland Place as if by Amerigo's conjuration, "turning up for him at the very climax of his special inner vision" (1:296). As she and the Prince stand facing one another, they each realize, through some simultaneous silent impulse, that they will become clandestine lovers.

> It was as if he then knew on the spot why he had been feeling for hours in such fashion—as if he in fact knew within the minute things he hadn't known even while she was panting, from the effect of the staircase, at the door of the room. He knew at the same time, none the less, that *she* knew still more

than he—in the sense, that is, of all the signs and portents
that might count for them (1:297).

"You knew . . . you knew today I'd come," Charlotte avows moments later, "And if you knew that you knew everything"
(1:301). Soon, their clairvoyant awareness of one another grows
so intense that simply being in the same room together for fleeting
intervals becomes "a workable substitute for contact." "They had
prolongations of instants that counted as visions of bliss; they had
slow approximations that counted as long caresses. The quality of
these passages in truth made the spoken word, and especially the
spoken word about other people, fall below them . . ." (1:339).

As with Kate and Densher, the climax of Charlotte and
Amerigo's "common consciousness" occurs just prior to the sexual
consummation of their love. In both relationships, telepathic sensitivity increases with sexual desire. When Charlotte informs Mrs.
Assingham that Amerigo and she are delaying their departure
from Matcham, the Prince finds that "practically without words,
without any sort of straight telegraphy" she has read his mind and
"uttered the exact plea that he had been keeping ready for the
same foreseen necessity" (1:345). As Amerigo strolls along the
terrace the next morning, Charlotte suddenly appears at an upper
window "as if she had been called by the pausing of his feet on the
flags" (1:355). Although the Prince has had no chance "such as he
needed, to speak the definite word to her," Charlotte has envisioned the excursion to Gloucester that he had wished to propose.

> They had these identities of impulse—they had had them re-
> peatedly before; and if such unarranged but unerring encoun-
> ters gave the measure of the degree in which people were, in
> the common phrase, meant for each other, no union in the
> world had ever been more sweetened with rightness . . . they
> were conscious of the same necessity at the same moment,
> only it was she who as a general thing most clearly saw her
> way to it. Something in her long look now out of the old grey
> window, something in the very poise of her hat, the colour of

her necktie, the prolonged stillness of her smile, touched into sudden light for him all the wealth of the fact that he could count on her (1:356).

Like their predecessors in *The Wings of the Dove*, the ultimate price that Charlotte and Amerigo must pay for their "occult" union is a complete submergence of their individual identities in one another. The imagery in which James describes their relationship implies a self-annihilating impulse at work from the beginning of the affair—the kiss that initially seals their union as lovers is figured forth as a mutual dissolution of being:

> "It's sacred," he said at last. "It's sacred," she breathed back to him. They vowed it, gave it out and took it in, drawn, by their intensity, more deeply together. Then of a sudden, through this tightened circle, as at the issue of a narrow strait into the sea beyond, everything broke up, broke down, gave way, melted and mingled. Their lips sought their lips, their pressure their response and their response their pressure; with a violence that had sighed itself the next moment to the longest and deepest stillnesses they passionately sealed their pledge (1:312).

We find here, perhaps, the most intensely lyrical passage Henry James ever wrote. Like a strait pouring into the sea, and like the growing passion of the lovers reaching a climax, the slow-rising cadences of James' prose suddenly give way to a final unpunctuated flow of words. Linguistic order seems to dissolve with the physical and spiritual melting together of the couple. So inextricable is this fusion that James abandons the personal pronouns "his" and "her" and speaks of both lovers in the plural—"their lips sought their lips." "Pressure" and "response" become indistinguishable as individualities break down, merge, and mingle. In a manner reminiscent of Swinburne, James chooses metaphors that are resonant both of sexual lovemaking and of death: "the tightened circle," "the narrow strait" issuing into "the sea beyond," the sudden passionate breakthrough into a vast "stillness."

Losing oneself in love, James believed, was a kind of death, for to lose one's vital sense of otherness, to submerge one's vision and will in a lover's, was to destroy one's capacity to respond to other centers of consciousness in the external world.

Just as Kate and Densher, through their "practical fusion of consciousness," mistakenly envisioned Milly as an innocent little girl, Charlotte and the Prince fix Maggie and her father in the unchanging images of children. Maggie is "a little dancing girl at rest, ever so light of movement, but most often panting gently, even a shade compunctiously, on a bench." Adam is "a little boy shyly entertaining in virtue of some imposed rank," an "infant king." Together, "they were good children, bless their hearts" going about in "the state of our primitive parents before the Fall" (1:334-335). In Maggie's case, these images are a fatal distortion, for, if Adam, in his "sweet simplicity," lives up to the role of his prelapsarian namesake, his daughter takes more from the Tree of Knowledge than any of James' other heroines. When James' lovers come to view the world through a single pair of eyes, perceived reality becomes nothing more than a series of arrested impressions, an impalpable dreamscape generated by their united consciousness. We find this phenomenon occurring at a party prior to their weekend in the country.

> It was impossible that [the Prince] shouldn't now and again meet Charlotte's eyes, as it was also visible that she now and again met her husband's. For her as well, in all his pulses, he felt the conveyed impression. It put them, it kept them together, through the vain show of their separation; made the two other faces, made the whole lapse of the evening, the people, the lights, the flowers, the pretended talk, the exquisite music, a mystic golden bridge between them, strongly swaying and sometimes almost vertiginous, for that intimacy (1:325).

For Charlotte and Amerigo, no less than for the narrator of *The Sacred Fount*, reality has come to consist of nothing more than what the inquiring mind (or united minds) wishes to see. Maggie and Adam become mere "faces," whose conscious presence makes no deeper impression than the lights, flowers, or music.

The failure of relationship in *The Golden Bowl* is really a failure of perception, an inability to recognize and sympathize with more than one center of consciousness. Charlotte's remark to Amerigo at the beginning of their affair explains its eventual collapse: "I can't put myself into Maggie's skin—I can't, as I say. It's not my fit—I shouldn't be able, as I see it, to breathe in it" (1:311). Whatever Maggie's shortcomings may be as a sexual lover, her unique triumph in the novel lies in her ability to put herself in Charlotte's skin, to think as she thinks and view her husband as she views him. She is able to win the Prince's love because she is capable of understanding Charlotte through her love for her husband. Before Maggie can fully fathom Amerigo or his lover, however, she must liberate herself from an all-absorbing union with her father.

When James first sketched the plot for *The Golden Bowl* in 1892, he recognized that the "necessary basis" for the entire work would have to be "an intense and exceptional degree of attachment between the father and daughter—he peculiarly paternal, she passionately filial."[5] During the twelve years that elapsed between this initial notebook entry and the composition of the novel, James' developing sense of the individual need for self-definition in love led him to modify his original conception. Although Adam and Maggie Verver's relationship unfolds "peculiarly" and "passionately," it involves something more than normal "paternal" and "filial" affection. After *The Wings of the Dove*, James realized that the only way in which his heroine might escape self-dissolution in love would be by establishing more than one vital circuit of relationship. As we have seen successively in the cases of Kate and Densher, Densher and Milly, and Charlotte and Amerigo, these telepathic circuits can be generated only by an extraordinary intensity of romantic love. It follows that, if Maggie was to have the capacity for maintaining her individual identity by virtue of multiple relationships, she would have to feel a romantic attachment for at least two different men. This kind of arrangement does not lie very comfortably alongside our western ideal of marital fidelity, an ideal that James was no more ready to relinquish in 1904 than he had been in 1881. Although James could deeply sympathize with the extramarital loves of Madame de Vionnet, Amerigo, and Charlotte—not to mention Edith Wharton's real life affair—adultery does not befit a Jamesian protagonist. For James, marriage and engagement were not simply agreements, but sacred vows. Densher, even after he has fallen in love with a dead image, is willing to honor his marital promise to Kate if she will wed him without Milly's money. Within the framework of marriage, it seems that the only person a Jamesian hero or heroine might deeply love, apart from a wife or husband, would be a close relative. What emerged in *The Golden Bowl* from this limitation was a second romantic attachment disguising itself in a father-daughter relationship.

If James was able to present Maggie's attraction to her father "without pondering it as an abnormality," as F. O. Matthiessen suggests,[6] he certainly invites his readers to do so. And, if Leon Edel is correct in observing that Victorian daughters were expected to be devoted to their fathers and to sacrifice their own interests,[7] it should also be noted that Victorian wives were expected to devote themselves, first and foremost, to their husbands. Maggie's inability to balance these two kinds of love, or fully to separate them, cannot be explained away in historical terms. If we accept Fanny Assingham's conventional explanation of Maggie's relationships, we must ignore one of the most compelling love triangles in all of James' fiction. "I quite hold," Fanny asseverates, "that a person can mostly feel but one passion—one *tender* passion, that is—at a time. Only that doesn't hold good for our primary and instinctive attachments, the 'voice of blood,' such as one's feeling for a parent or brother. Those may be intense and yet not prevent other intensities . . ." (1:395).

In truth, James' presentation of Maggie demonstrates that one *can* feel more than one "tender passion" at a time, and that the distinction between romantic and filial love is not always a clear

one. In describing Adam and Maggie's relationship, he repeatedly
speaks of the pair, not as father and daughter, but as husband and
wife. Since the death of the first Mrs. Verver, Adam has come to
see Maggie in the role of her mother. James' heroine is so eager to
conform to this image that she not only waits upon her father like
an attendant wife, but dresses for him and even wears "her hair
down very straight and flat over her temples, in the constant manner of her mother" (1:188). In urging her father to remarry,
Maggie herself explains: "It was as if you couldn't be in the mar-
ket when you were married to *me*. Or rather as if I kept people off,
innocently, by being married to you. Now that I'm married to
someone else you're, as in consequence, married to nobody"
(1:172). Ironically, of course, Maggie remains spiritually wedded
to Adam; her marriage with the Prince only draws her closer to
her father, and the birth of her first child, which would ordinarily
"take its place as a new link between a wife and a husband," is
converted instead "into a link between a mamma and a grandpapa"
(1:156).

Freud points out that it is typical for little girls to have fantasies
about being married to their fathers, and that, although this attachment may appear innocent, it actually springs from an underlying sexual source. By clinging to their fathers, such girls
"conceal their libido under an affection which may manifest itself
without self-reproach." Freud explains that this attraction becomes a type of neurosis when, like Maggie's, it persists beyond
adolescence:

Many persons are detained at each of the stations in the
course of development through which the individual must
pass; and accordingly there are persons who never overcome
the parental authority and never, or very imperfectly, withdraw their affection from their parents. They are mostly girls,
who, to the delight of their parents retain their full infantile
love far beyond puberty, and it is instructive to find that in
their married life these girls are incapable of fulfilling their

duties to their husbands. They make cold wives and remain
sexually anesthetic. This shows that the apparently nonsexual
love for parents and sexual love are nourished from the same
source.[8]

James could embody this kind of relationship in *The Golden Bowl*
without giving it a name, just as he could understand Olive Chancellor's lesbianism in *The Bostonians* and the corruption of children in *The Turn of the Screw* without explicitly identifying them.

Unlike many of the novelists who have followed him, James also
manages to represent sexual inadequacy without taking us into his
heroine's bedroom. Although Amerigo has a child by Maggie, he
perpetually thinks of her as a prepubescent child and turns to
Charlotte for sexual fulfillment. Similarly, Charlotte's passionate
attraction to the Prince is urged, in part, by Mr. Verver's failure as
a sexual lover. Her sad explanation to Amerigo, "It's not, at any
rate, my fault," speaks volumes about the desperate state of her
marriage. Maggie is the only character in the novel to view Adam
as a mature man, while Adam ambiguously thinks of his daughter
as a cross between "a nymph" and "a nun" (1:188). The images
suggest a peculiar mixture not simply of paganism and Christianity, but of innocence and budding maturity, of chastity and shy
nubility. "Nymphs and nuns," James observes, "were certainly
separate types,"—but so too, we recall, are wives and daughters.
Adam can contentedly combine these images in his imagination
because Maggie strives to combine spousal and filial roles in life.

Although Freudian explanations help to illuminate Maggie's relationship with her father, the quality of her love and the refinement of her consciousness take her beyond the proscribed limits of
a simple Electra complex. Like Charlotte and Amerigo, Maggie
and Adam have risen to a telepathic oneness of thought and feeling
through their attachment: "They could be silent together, at any
time, beautifully, with much more comfort than hurriedly expres-
sive. It appeared indeed to have become true that their common
appeal measured itself for vividness just by this economy of
sound" (2:77). Shortly after Maggie's marriage, they simulta-

neously sense, through a "mute communication" (1:155), the growing danger of fortune huntresses like Mrs. Rance. In a single glance, they each recognize that Maggie's marriage has left Adam alone and conspicuously without a wife.

> They had made vacant by their marriage his immediate fore-ground, his personal precinct—they being the Princess and the Prince. They had made room in it for others—so others had become aware. He became aware himself, for that matter, during the minute Maggie stood before speaking; and with the sense moreover of what he saw her see, he had the sense of what she saw *him* (1:154).

Ostensibly, Maggie arranges her father's marriage with Char-lotte to save him from his loneliness—and, ostensibly, Adam weds to free his daughter from her sense of responsibility toward him. Once again, however, the conscious motives of James' characters disguise deeper, unacknowledged desires: instead of relieving the emotional interdependency of father and daughter, Adam's mar-riage knits them more tightly together. The addition of a socially active, self-reliant fourth member to their group assures that Amerigo will not go neglected and so frees Maggie and Adam to act as a couple once again. Mrs. Assingham attributes this "oppo-site effect" of Adam's marriage to an "extraordinary perversity" of fortune, by which "mutual consideration, all round" creates a "bottomless gulf" (1:394). Although the peculiar pairing off of father and daughter, mother-in-law and son-in-law clearly arises from a combination of interests, it results more from unstated complementary self-interests than from any conscious altruism. If James' characters have "a benefactor in common," as Amerigo senses, it is probably the united power of their own unconscious wills.

While Adam and Maggie's consanguineous intimacy was apt to raise a few Edwardian eyebrows, the crippling flaw in their rela-tionship is the same one that ruins the more conventional loves of Kate and Densher, Charlotte and Amerigo. Maggie herself ex-presses it succinctly when she remarks to her father: "The thing is

CHAPTER SIX

. . . that I don't think we lead, as regards other people, any life at all" (1:175). Because they exist only for one another, Maggie and Adam, like Charlotte and Amerigo, make the ever-changing, living continuum outside conform to a series of pictures in their united imagination. For the first half of the novel, Maggie sees Amerigo, through her father's eyes, as a splendid antique artifact, "a rarity, an object of beauty, an object of a price" (1:12). On the eve of their marriage, she explains to the Prince that she has not fallen in love with "what you call your unknown quantity, your particular self," but with "the generations behind you, the follies and the crimes, the plunder and the waste—the wicked Pope, the monster most of all, whom so many volumes in your family library are all about" (1:9-10). Remarkably, Maggie senses from the outset that she is almost willfully blinding herself to her husband's "particular" identity as a human being. Her remark to her father, "I don't *want* to know. . . . There are things that are sacred—whether they're joys or pains" (1:187), goes far in explaining both her initial failure to understand Amerigo and her slowness in suspecting his affair with Charlotte. This innate fear of mature knowledge draws Maggie into an ever-deepening, self-dissolving relationship with Adam, who views the world through the eyes of an innocent, if rather acquisitive, child. Unlike Charlotte and the Prince, however, Maggie and Adam do not share a "perfect parity of imagination," and, in time, the finely tuned consciousness of James' heroine responds uncontrollably to external vibrations that are too subtle for her father. The highest accomplishment of Maggie's developing consciousness is her unique capacity for subliminally loving two men at once, for fully understanding two distinct centers of awareness.

Maggie's mature love for the Prince comes upon a sudden wave of clairvoyant understanding that is triggered by an image recalled from the past. In much the same way that Amerigo's telepathic love for Charlotte returns when she brings to life a buried memory picture, Maggie comes to a complete love and understanding of her husband when she recalls the expression he wore on his return from Matcham. Her "immense little memory of him arrested at the door" springs back the next morning when she sees the same "physiognomic light" (2:103), the same expression of surprise, playing across Charlotte's gaze. This momentary glimpse functions for Maggie in much the same way that the tea-dipped madeleine does for Proust's Marcel: it is a link between conscious and unconscious awareness, a one-dimensional portal that suddenly expands into incalculable depths of perception and sensation. From a "kinship of expression," Maggie reads a kinship of minds. She thinks of Charlotte and the Prince as a two-sided medallion whose figured images are turned in upon one another and realizes that their minds have long been operating in a mystical harmony.

> The word for it, the word that flashed the light, was that they were *treating* her, that they were proceeding with her—and for that matter with her father—by a plan that was the exact counterpart of her own. It wasn't from her that they took their cue, but—and this was what in particular made her sit up—from each other; and with a depth of unanimity, an exact coincidence of inspiration, that when once her attention had begun to fix to it struck her as staring out at her in recovered identities of behavior, expression and tone (2:41-42).

As Mrs. Assingham notes, Maggie's discovery "isn't a question of belief or of proof," but of "natural perception" (2:131)—but what is natural in James' heroine would be supernatural in almost anyone else. Her love for Amerigo is so potent that, like Milly Theale, she is able to read not only her lover's mind, but that of his mistress as well. After making Amerigo aware of her suspicions, Maggie intuitively knows that he will not tell Charlotte, and, beneath the smooth surface of their daily intercourse, she eavesdrops upon their tormented, silent conversations.

> She saw [Charlotte], face to face with the Prince, take from him the chill of his stiffest admonition, with the possibilities of deeper difficulty that it represented for each. She heard her ask, irritated and somber, what tone, in God's name—since her bravery didn't suit him—she *was* then to adopt; and by

way of a fantastic flight of divination she heard Amerigo reply, in a voice of which every fine note, familiar and admirable, came home to her, that one must really manage such
prudences a little oneself (2:282).

Maggie's love for Amerigo triumphs over Charlotte's because it
inspires what she modestly calls "some imagination of the states
of others"—not simply *another*, but the Prince, Charlotte, and
Adam all at once. Through her understanding of Amerigo, Maggie
penetrates Charlotte's associated consciousness; she knows how
her rival will think and behave because "for certain passages . . .
she absolutely looked with Charlotte's grave eyes" (2:283). The
Prince shifts his love from Charlotte to Maggie as he becomes
aware of his wife's superior consciousness, and, by the end of the
novel, he realizes that Charlotte's fatal flaw is her failure of sympathy. "She ought to have *known* you," he tells Maggie, "She
ought to have understood you better" (2:347). By virtue of her
double love, James' heroine can, in one moment, read Charlotte's
thoughts through the mind of her husband and, in another, with a
"sharp identity of emotion" (2:292), compassionately watch her
through the eyes of Mr. Verver. The most remarkable part of this
phenomenon is that Maggie's love for Amerigo neither usurps nor
alters in kind her love for her father. Unlike Lawrence's *Sons and
Lovers*, in which Paul Morel becomes capable of a mature passion
only by bitterly repudiating his mother, *The Golden Bowl* poses an
Oedipal triangle only to seek a reconciliation within it. Nevertheless, it is appropriate that James' last important novel and Lawrence's first, separated by less than a decade, should both consider
the possibilities of a twofold love, for Lawrence, like James, eventually came to sense that no single relationship could permanently
define individual identity.

Through her extraordinary psychic sympathy, Maggie becomes
the first and only Jamesian character to transcend the self-
obliterating fusion of single love and to establish multiple circuits
of relationship. She escapes both the constrictive prison of the ego
and the dissolution of self in another by recognizing two distinct
centers of consciousness through two equal loves. The loftiest ideal

of love in all of James' fiction finds expression when Maggie explains to Fanny why she can "bear anything."

> "Oh, bear!" Mrs. Assingham fluted. "For love," said the Princess. Fanny hesitated. "Of your father?" "For Love," Maggie repeated. It kept her friend watching. "Of your husband?" "For love," Maggie said again (2:116).

By refusing to devote herself exclusively to one person, Maggie transforms love from a personal sentiment into a kind of religion. Rather than diminishing one another, her two loves grow more intense, more perfectly defined, by virtue of their coexistence. The diversity of her devotion only increases her capacity to love.

Although Maggie embodies James' purest vision of what the human heart is capable of, she cannot realize her own dream: "the golden bowl—as it *was* to have been. . . . The bowl with all our happiness in it. The bowl without the crack" (2:216-217). Few symbols in modern fiction have been so variously and inextricably woven into the fabric of a novel as this vessel of crystal and gold. Like the occult symbols of Yeats' poetry, its meanings proliferate, change, and deepen as the work unfolds. In its simplest terms, the fractured bowl is intended to represent both the deeply flawed love of Amerigo and Charlotte and the evil that Maggie discovers lurking beneath the immaculate surface of her married life. In a broader sense, however, it becomes an emblem for "the latent crack" in each relationship in the novel—even the final union of Maggie and Amerigo. The movement of the golden bowl through the novel from Charlotte's hands to Maggie's anticipates their successive possession of the Prince's love. Although Amerigo seems a "pure and perfect crystal," he warns from the beginning that crystals "sometimes have cracks and flaws" (1:139) and is the first to detect the fissure in the bowl. Later in the novel, James implies a common weakness in Amerigo's relationships with both Charlotte and Maggie by interweaving the imagery of gold. In particular, the Prince compares his day in the country with Charlotte to "a great gold cup that we must somehow drain together" (1:359), and Maggie picks this image up immediately upon his return when she speaks of "the full cup of her need for him." All of the bowl's symbolic resonances unite in the climactic scene in which Fanny Assingham, insisting that nothing stands between Maggie and the Prince, dashes it to the floor. Maggie's act of gathering up the three broken pieces and holding them together in her hands has customarily been interpreted as her attempt to salvage general happiness out of the love triangle in which she, Amerigo, and Charlotte are embroiled. If we consider the other love triangle in the novel, however—the struggle in Maggie's mind to reconcile father-love and husband-love—her attempt to join together the shattered bowl becomes a splendid symbol for the perfectly balanced double love that she longs to maintain. Like the "solid detached foot" that was made to support the two "almost equal parts" of the cup, Maggie is capable of sustaining two vital relationships. Her ideal of love, like the golden bowl, is incomplete and unbalanced if one part is missing.

The hidden flaw that fractures the love relationships in *The Wings of the Dove* and *The Golden Bowl* is, paradoxically, man's instinctive yearning for fusion with one other human being. At the end of James' final novel, Maggie longs to maintain a perfectly polarized double love, but neither the Prince, nor Adam, nor Charlotte, nor society at large is able to share or accept this kind of arrangement. In a world of Maggie Ververs, an individual might define his identity through multiple love relationships, but, as James realized, Maggie's capacity for love is unique, and her ideals are incompatible with society's. Like Rupert Birkin, who feels the need for a second circuit of relationship at the end of *Women in Love*, Maggie is finally frustrated by our culture's insistence upon single-minded devotion in marriage. Ursula's answer to Birkin is, effectively, society's answer to Maggie: "You can't have two kinds of love." Maggie realizes that Amerigo, as a husband, can fully love her only if she severs herself from her father and lavishes her love exclusively upon him. Although she encourages her father to leave her, she regards his departure for American City as a forced separation. "We're the ones who are lost," she observes, "Lost to each other—father and I . . . lost to each other much more really than Amerigo and Charlotte are; since for them it's just, it's right, it's deserved, while for us it's only sad and strange and not caused by our fault" (2:333). Maggie is, perhaps, a bit too eager to exonerate herself and Adam. If she had loved Amerigo with a mature passion before their marriage, she might have had a better chance of balancing the conflicting claims of husband and father. Mr. Verver, for his part, is no less guilty of failing as a husband than Charlotte is of failing as a wife; and he is far more deserving than Charlotte of the Prince's charge of being "stupid."

While the Adam Verver's are finally condemned to the exile of one another's company, Maggie and Amerigo face a more uncertain fate. If they are not quite left in what R. P. Blackmur takes to be "the horrible adultery of incompatible isolation,"[9] neither are they on the verge of a redemptive marital love, as Quentin Anderson and Leon Edel, among others, suggest. James' prince and princess have learned to love one another with a frightening intensity, frightening because, detached from the rest of the world as they are at the close of the novel, their passion must inevitably consume their individual identities. As Amerigo holds Maggie in his arms in the book's final scene, his words underscore their absolute isolation in one another: ". . . close to her, her face kept before him, his hands holding her shoulders, his whole act enclosing her, he presently echoed: 'See? I see nothing but *you*.' " The words fill Maggie with terror, for she has come to realize that a lover who sees nothing beyond his beloved ultimately longs to absorb the beloved's consciousness. *The Golden Bowl* concludes in an atmosphere of emotional claustrophobia and despair; the lovers draw closer together until their embrace ends in a kind of blackout. "And the truth of it had with this force after a moment so strangely lighted his eyes that as for pity and dread of them she buried her own in his breast" (2:368-369). Like the kiss that sealed Amerigo's love for Charlotte, this final embrace, which seals his love for Maggie, suggests a blind self-obliterating fusion. In her sorrow, Maggie surrenders herself completely to her husband, as she had once surrendered herself to her father. The merging of identities, which destroyed Amerigo's relationship with Charlotte and which kept Maggie for so long a solitary prisoner of her father's love, seems the only possible destiny for James' prince and princess. The novel's closing image implicitly links Maggie's marriage with the darkness of death—the death of her individual identity and the burial of her consciousness in that of her husband.

By the end of *The Golden Bowl*, James realized that, if love was ever to establish personal identity, it would have to transform not simply the individual consciousness, but the consciousness of an entire culture. Maggie Verver might realize her ideal of self only in a society where universal sympathy replaced emotional greed, where lovers remained in dynamic contact with the living world outside instead of creating an inner world of their own, where marriage was regarded as a sacred relation, but not the only relation. It is no less difficult to imagine how such a society might come about today than it was in James' lifetime, and, as the novelist passed into old age, he could but look at the failure of love, the ubiquity of self-interest, and the waste of human life all around him and shriek with bitterness.

The handful of stories that James wrote after *The Golden Bowl* bear witness to his pessimism. They are inhabited by spiritual nomads, enervated men and women who possess neither a sense of individual identity nor the capacity to love. Each story presents a character locked hopelessly within himself, making feeble attempts to communicate with another soul. Much of the horror that James expresses in these final tales has its immediate source in his return to New York after a twenty-one-year absence. If the European society of his late novels had been corrupt, its vulgarities and vices could scarcely be compared to those that he confronted in the American of 1904. Following Adam Verver back to his native land after the completion of *The Golden Bowl*, James found the "American gregarious ideal" had produced a society of avaricious solipsists. Much of *The American Scene*, the book of impressions that was to emerge from his visit, reads like a gloss upon a line in his final tale: "There was nothing like a crowd . . . for making one feel lonely."[10] To the novelist's eyes, the "whole costly up-town demonstration" of New York's gleaming architecture seemed merely "a record of individual loneliness."[11] Like the London of Eliot's *The Waste Land*, James' New York is an "unreal city," lost in the blur of disconnected activity and barren of love. In paragraph after paragraph, he throws before our eyes kaleidoscopic images of a civilization at once mechanical and chaotic, a sprawling, impersonal fragmented metropolis where pecuniary power "beat its wings in the void." Visions of confusion abound, from the "multitudinous skyscrapers" of the Manhattan skyline sticking "like extravagant pins in a cushion already overplanted, stuck as in the dark, anywhere and anyhow," to the "great intricate frenzied dance, half merry, half desperate," of water traffic in New York harbor, to the breakdown of American speech into "a mere helpless slobber of disconnected vowel sounds."[12]

Returning to the city of his birth, James found himself a stranger in a society of strangers. Like the hero of *Le Temps retrouvé*, he could stare out at a world transformed by time beyond his recognition and write: "There was no escape from the ubiquitous alien into the future, or even into the present; there was an escape but into the past." For James, however, even the vestiges of the past—the Washington Square of his childhood—contained acute reminders of the alien present. Upon finding a "high, square, impersonal structure" towering over his family house, he had the sense "of being amputated of half my history."[13] The protagonists whom James created in the years following *The American Scene* share this sense of alienation both from society and from their past selves. They exist like so many furtive fish swimming, each alone in the airtight aquarium of its own consciousness. Nowhere is this solitude more oppressive than in "The Bench of Desolation" (1909), whose hero, Herbert Dodd, "had nowhere to carry, to deposit, or contentedly let loose and lock up . . . his swollen consciousness, which fairly split in twain the raw shell of his sordid little boarding-place" (p. 412). Cut off from the rest of mankind, Dodd's ego seems to extend from horizon to horizon: "The arch of the sky and the spread of the sea and shore alone gave him space; he could roam with himself anywhere, in short, far or near . . ." (p. 413). Sued for not marrying his first fiancée, forced to mortgage his secondhand bookstore, and left a widower by his wife's early death, he has been reduced to a state of such passive self-absorption that he can but watch the continual transformations of his identity. Shambling down the street, he seems engaged "in a fascinated study of the motions of his shadow, the more or less grotesque shape projected . . . over the blanched asphalt of the Parade . . . dangling and dancing . . ." (pp. 414-415). Under the pressure of time and poverty, Dodd spends most days sitting alone on a desolate bench overlooking the sea, meditating upon his misfortune. His one chance to break out of the chaotic sphere of his own ego comes with the return of his former fiancée, Kate Cookham, whom he had falsely suspected of infidelity. Only when Dodd thinks of her does "the dangling and dancing of his image [give] way to perfect immobility" (p. 415). Kate, for reasons all her own, still loves him and has kept all the money that he once paid her just so she might save him from his poverty and loneliness. Dodd, however, hasn't the emotional strength to liberate himself from isolation by meeting her as a lover. When they meet by the seaside bench at the end of the story, Dodd lets Kate put her arm around him, but he knows that, far from saving him from himself, "she was beside him on the bench of desolation" (p. 425).

"Fordham Castle" (1904) and "Julia Bride" (1908) present similar visions of faceless characters trapped in hopeless isolation. In the earlier tale, Abel Taker, a social failure at forty-five, has changed his name to C. P. Addard at the insistence of his domineering wife, who is making her way into English society under an assumed name of her own. Abandoned in a Geneva pension, Taker finds one name as meaningless as another and wishes he could dissolve out of life altogether—until he meets a fellow sufferer, Mrs. Vanderplank. This lady, Taker soon discovers, is really Mrs. Magaw, whose society-seeking daughter has imposed a series of name changes upon her like the ones Mrs. Taker has imposed upon him. Taker finds an unprecedented "foretaste of felicity" just hanging "in the iridescent ether with Mrs. Vanderplank, to whom he wasn't insignificant" (p. 142), and, by the end of the tale, he considers the possibility of establishing at least a nominal identity by virtue of the relationship. "Abel Taker's in his grave," he tells his friend. "You're conversing with C. P. Addard. *He* may be alive—but even this I don't know yet . . . I'm trying him, Mrs. Magaw, on you" (p. 140). Like Herbert Dodd, however, Taker is destined to remain in his desolation. Despite his affection, he makes no real contact with Mrs. Magaw, who questions his sanity as she leaves for England at her daughter's beckoning. As he puts her on the train, Taker feels "left in his solitude, to the sense of his extinction," but faces it without protest. The story ends with his reflection, "Why certainly I'm dead" (p. 149).

Taker is a spiritual counterpart of the radiantly pretty Julia Bride, who finds it equally impossible to establish a defining love relationship. Jilted in her engagements to six different suitors, each of whom has discovered her mother's three divorces, she is doomed to live in a society that admires her only as a beautiful ornament. With each prospective engagement, Julia must adopt a new role to hide her past. Love has become a vicious parlor game in which social climbers trade partners at will, cheat and deceive, "snatch and scramble." Some characters, like Julia, play the game out of desperation and with a sense of their own ruin; others, like Amy Evans of "The Velvet Glove," play willingly and with every expectation of success. When the writer-protagonist of this story, John Berridge, meets Amy at a party, he imagines her a "Princess" and his hopes for romance run high when she takes him on a long night drive through Paris. Berridge, a perpetual observer of life and creator of fictional fantasies, longs for a woman who lives the experiences about which he can only write. What he discovers instead, at the end of their ride, is an authoress of trashy novels who dwells as much in the sequestered realm of the imagination as he does. When he learns that the beautiful Amy's real motive in getting him alone has been to persuade him to write an influential preface to her latest romance, he can only ineffectually protest, "You *are* Romance. . . . Your preface . . . was written long years ago by the most beautiful imagination of man" (p. 263). By the end of this perfectly etched little tale, however, it has become clear that there can be no genuine romance in the world of these characters, for there is no real love.

Among the characters of James' last tales, only Spencer Brydon of "The Jolly Corner" (1908) searches for his identity with genuine intensity. Returning to his New York birthplace after long years in Europe, as James himself had done four years earlier in 1904, Brydon is consumed with curiosity about what he would have been like had he remained in America and used his incipient business talents to participate in the economic revolution. He senses that he can track down this other self, and the deserted family mansion becomes the setting for his nightly peregrinations down the road not taken. Like Ralph Pendrel, Brydon stalks an alter ego that represents not simply a self that might have been, but an unconscious part of his total identity. One night, Brydon succeeds where Dodd, Taker, and Berridge cannot—he momentarily escapes his conscious ego—but he finds the ravaged other self that looms up at him from inside the front door too horrible to acknowledge. When the cowering specter raises its "grizzled bent head" to reveal its face, Brydon feels that "the bared identity was too hideous as *his*" (p. 225), and faints dead away as the figure moves toward him. He wakes to find his head resting in the lap of Alice Staverton, who saw his alter ego in a dream at the exact moment he did. Alice is the last of James' telepathic females, and, like May Bartram, she is willing to accept anything in the man she loves—even his devastated doppelgänger. Brydon's terrifying self-confrontation, however, has rendered him incapable of ever again transcending his conscious isolation and meeting Alice at her level of clairvoyant love. He cannot become fully aware of another unless he accepts full awareness of himself. As Brydon draws Alice to his breast at the end of the story and hears her whisper consolingly, "And he isn't—no, he isn't—*you*" (p. 232), he resembles not so much a romantic lover as a frightened child seeking his mother's comfort after a nightmare.

Perhaps no other tale so captures the nightmare that James himself experienced in New York as his last complete work of fiction,

"A Round of Visits" (1910). The title itself suggests the absurd circularity of human pursuits in James' last tales, the inability of men and women to form any genuine bonds of love. Human relationships are themselves little more than visits, as characters inevitably return to the isolated condition in which they began. Mark Monteith returns to America after a few years abroad to learn that Phil Bloodgood, the friend to whom he has entrusted his funds, has absconded as a swindler. As Monteith wanders forlornly around New York, "hovering now and then at vague crossways, radiations of roads to nothing" (p. 437), he finds that he has lost not only his fortune, but also "all the broken bits of the past, the loose ends of old relationships, that he had supposed he might pick up again" (p. 437). Haunting the drawing rooms of his old friends in search of sympathy, he finds himself an outsider listening to the woes of others. Only when he decides to visit Newton Winch, an unpleasant former acquaintance who is reportedly depressed and sick, does Monteith understand that, by extending his sympathy to someone even less fortunate than himself, he might be saved from his morbid self-absorption, "the obsession of egotism." He finds Winch transformed from an ordinary fellow into one who has been made keenly sensitive through his suffering. As they discuss Bloodgood, Monteith is filled with a strange compassion for the man who has swindled him. There arises in his mind "a vision of his old friend hunted and at bay" (p. 450), and he asks Winch to consider the remorse that Bloodgood must feel. Almost like Maggie Verver, Monteith seems momentarily capable of putting himself in another's skin, but the bitter irony of James' final tale is that this outpouring of sympathy destroys rather than redeems. Winch, like Bloodgood, has been guilty of larceny and is waiting for the authorities, with a gun nearby, when his visitor arrives. In compassionately reflecting upon his friend's suffering and guilt, Monteith inadvertently presents to Winch an image of the misery his own dishonesty has likewise caused. The victim's forgiveness only heightens the criminal's self-hatred. As Monteith leaves, he meets the police entering Winch's apartment and hears, a moment later, the crack of a discharged pistol. When the police criticize

Monteith for not preventing the suicide, he realizes that the burden of guilt is now his own and replies: "I really think I must practically have caused it" (p. 459).

Taken together, the stories that follow *The Golden Bowl* are an illustration of Prince Amerigo's mature wisdom: "Everything's terrible, cara—in the heart of man." In the murky dawn of the twentieth century, James seems, for the first time, to despair that love might ever free man from the troubled abyss of his own mind. Unlike the protagonists of these final tales, however, James himself did not wish for the extinction of consciousness. Rather, as he approached the end of his life, he labored, in a manner much like Yeats, to give a kind of final form to his life and art. In the New York edition of his works, which he scrupulously selected and edited, beginning in 1907, and in the three volumes of autobiography that followed, James fixed his identity in history in a way that his characters had never been able to fix theirs in life. Even as he pored over the past, however, the novelist remained finely attuned to the ever-changing present. Man was isolated, he realized, love short-lived, and identity impossible to determine "under all the great ebbing, melting and irrevocableness of life," but one had to make the most of the prison of one's conscious awareness. Old and infirm and horrified at the approach of World War I, James could send Henry Adams a copy of *Notes of a Son and Brother* and still urge his old friend to live:

> Of *course* we are lone survivors, of course the past that was our lives is at the bottom of an abyss—if the abyss *has* any bottom; of course, too, there's no use talking unless one particularly *wants* to. But the purpose, almost, of my printed divagations was to show you that one *can*, strange to say, still want to—or can at least behave as if one did. Behold me therefore so behaving—and apparently capable of continuing to do so. I still find my consciousness interesting—under *cultivation* of interest. Cultivate it *with* me, dear Henry—that's what I hoped to make you do—to cultivate yours for all it has in common with mine.[14]

FOR LOVE

For James the novelist, the cultivation of consciousness had always entailed the cultivation of love, and, several months after his letter to Adams, he sketched a love plot for his abandoned work, *The Sense of the Past*. Although Ralph Pendrel journeys out of the chaotic present into a remote time, he is to be redeemed only when he is brought back to the present through the telepathic power of Aurora Coyne's love. Had James lived to finish the novel, it is difficult to imagine how his lovers might have overcome the psychological and social obstacles to identity that confront Maggie Verver at the end of *The Golden Bowl*. As we have seen, however, James' vision of love evolved continually throughout his career, and, as he undertook a love story in the twilight of his life, we may imagine the Master reflecting upon his own advice of years before: "Never say you know the last word about any human heart."

NOTES

Preface

[1] Van Wyck Brooks, *The Pilgrimage of Henry James*, p. 105.

[2] Maxwell Geismar, *Henry James and the Jacobites*, p. 436.

[3] James Thurber, *Lanterns and Lances*, p. 103.

[4] Naomi Lebowitz, *The Imagination of Loving*, p. 66.

[5] Lisa Appignanesi, *Femininity and the Creative Imagination*, p. 22.

[6] Martha Banta, *Henry James and the Occult*, pp. 154-163.

ONE: The Great Relation

[1] Edith Wharton, *A Backward Glance*, pp. 172-173.

[2] Lionel Trilling observes in his essay on *The Princess Casamassima*: "To be sure, the legend of James does not associate him with love; indeed, it is a fact symptomatic of the condition of American letters that Sherwood Anderson, a writer who himself spoke much of love, was able to say of James that he was the novelist of 'those who hate' [*The Liberal Imagination*, p. 86]."

[3] Leon Edel, Introduction to *Henry James: The Future of the Novel*, p. viii.

[4] Roger Gard, ed., *Henry James: The Critical Heritage*, p. 28.

[5] Ibid., p. 24.

[6] "Recent Literature," *Atlantic Monthly* 35 (April 1875):495; reprinted in Gard, p. 34.

[7] Gard, p. 40.

[8] "James' *Roderick Hudson*," *North American Review* 122 (April 1876):425; in Gard, p. 42.

[9] "Recent Literature," *Atlantic Monthly* 43 (February 1879):167-169; in Gard, pp. 72-73.

[10] Henry James (Charles Dickens') *"Our Mutual Friend,"* p. 787.

[11] "Reviews," *Literary World* 12 (December 1881):473; in Gard, p. 105.

[12] Ibid., p. 474.

[13] "Novels of the Week," *Athenaeum* 2658 (October 1878):431; in Gard, p. 53.

[14] "Reviews," *Literary World* 12 (December 1881):474.

[15] Gard, Introduction, p. 15.

[16] In Gard, p. 172.

[17] H. G. Wells, *Boon, The Mind of the Race, The Wild Asses of the Devil, and The Last Trump*, pp. 112-113.

[18] Ibid.

NOTES, CHAPTER ONE

[19] Arnold Bennett, *The Journals of Arnold Bennett*, vol. 1, edited by Newman Flower (London: Cassell, 1932), p. 206; in Gard, p. 373.

[20] Mark Twain, *Mark Twain—Howells Letters 1872-1910*, edited by H. N. Smith and William Gibson (Cambridge; Harvard University Press, 1960), p. 534.

[21] In Gard, p. 277.

[22] Frank Moore Colby, "The Queerness of Henry James," *Bookman* (America) 15 (June 1902):396-397; in Gard, pp. 335-337.

[23] Rebecca West, *Henry James*, p. 70.

[24] Ibid., pp. 107-108.

[25] André Gide (from an unsent letter to Charles Du Bos), reprinted in F. W. Dupee, ed., *The Question of Henry James*, p. 251.

[26] Lawrence, whose career was just beginning as James' was drawing to a close, mentioned him only in passing, while Hardy accused him of "saying nothing in infinite sentences" and fitly summed up his attitude in a remark to his wife: "He kept on writing . . . but I really wasn't interested."

[27] In Gard, p. 87.

[28] Henry James, *The Notebooks of Henry James*, p. 188.

[29] Henry James, "The Future of the Novel," in *The Future of the Novel*, p. 39.

[30] Henry James, *Notes on Novelists*, p. 237.

[31] James enunciates this belief most clearly in "The Art of Fiction" (1884), in *The Future of the Novel*.

[32] James, *Notes on Novelists*, p. 237.

[33] Henry James, *Autobiography*, p. 508f.

[34] Ibid., pp. 508-509.

[35] Ibid., p. 509.

[36] Ibid.

[37] Ibid., p. 283.

[38] Ibid., p. 509.

[39] Leon Edel, *Henry James: The Untried Years*, p. 228.

[40] Ibid., p. 326.

[41] Ibid., p. 234.

[42] James, *Autobiography*, p. 428f.

[43] Ibid., p. 8.

[44] Ibid., p. 16.

[45] Ibid., p. 17.

[46] Ibid., pp. 32-33.

[47] Ibid., p. 56.

[48] As Viola Hopkins Winner demonstrates in her book, *Henry James and the Visual Arts*, James occasionally used paintings as a center of dramatic focus. In the early tale, "The Madonna of the Future," he builds a scene around two men gazing at Raphael's "Madonna of the Chair," and, in *The Wings of the Dove*, Milly Theale recognizes her impending doom as she stares at Bronzino's portrait of Lucrezia.

[49] James, *Autobiography*, p. 63.

50 Ibid., p. 92.

51 Ibid., p. 62.

52 Ibid., pp. 46-47.

53 Henry James, from "The New Novel," originally titled "The Younger Generation," *Times Literary Supplement*, March 19 and April 2, 1914; reprinted in *The Future of the Novel*, p. 264.

54 Henry James, "The Lesson of Balzac," in *The Future of the Novel*, p. 100.

55 Henry James (review of George Sand), *Galaxy* 24 (July 1877):55.

56 Henry James (Emile Zola's) "Nana," *Parisian* (Paris) no. 48 (February 1880):9; reprinted in *The Future of the Novel*, p. 94.

57 Henry James, "Gabriele D'Annunzio," in *Henry James: Selected Literary Criticism*, edited by Morris Shapira (New York: Horizon Press, 1964), p. 295.

58 James, "Our Mutual Friend," p. 787.

59 Ibid.

60 Henry James, *Notes and Reviews*, p. 11.

61 Henry James, *The Art of the Novel*, p. 68.

62 Henry James, "The Novels of George Eliot," *Atlantic Monthly* 18 (October 1866):488, quoted by Cornelia Pulsifer Kelley, *The Early Development of Henry James*, p. 63.

63 James, "Our Mutual Friend," p. 787.

64 James, *Notes and Reviews*, p. 71.

TWO: A Sacred Terror

1 Henry James, "The Art of Fiction," in *The Future of the Novel*, p. 13.

2 William James, *Principles of Psychology*, vol. 1.

3 Henry James, *The Complete Tales of Henry James*, 2:227-228.

4 Henry James, *The Art of the Novel*, p. 46.

5 Walter Pater, *The Renaissance*, p. 157.

6 Graham Hough, *The Last Romantics*, p. 140.

7 Pater, p. 157.

8 James, "The Art of Fiction," p. 12.

9 James, *Autobiography*, p. 17.

10 Henry James, *Roderick Hudson*, p. 61.

11 Henry James, *The Painter's Eye*, p. 115.

12 Ibid., p. 114.

13 James, *Roderick Hudson*, p. 138.

14 James, *Complete Tales*, 2:244. All subsequent references are cited in text by volume and page.

15 James, *Roderick Hudson*, pp. 9-10.

16 James Kraft, *The Early Tales of Henry James*, p. 123.

17 Denis de Rougemont, *Love in the Western World*, p. 41.

18 Rougemont points out that the desire for earthly separation is central to all

courtly love. Tristram and Isolde, for example, "behave as if aware that whatever obstructs love must ensure and consolidate it in the heart of each and intensify it in the moment they reach the absolute obstacle, which is death," p. 41.

[19] James, *Autobiography*, p. 178.

[20] James, *The Painter's Eye*, p. 90.

[21] James, *Autobiography*, p. 148.

[22] Henry James, *The Letters of Henry James*, 1:17.

[23] One is also reminded of Thomas Hardy's well-known formulation, "Love lives on propinquity but dies of contact." Although James was never an admirer of Hardy's work, characters such as Eustacia Vye of *The Return of the Native* and Jocelyn Pierston of *The Well-Beloved* resemble his early protagonists more closely than any others in nineteenth-century fiction. As J. Hillis Miller explains in his penetrating study, *Thomas Hardy: Distance and Desire*, Hardy's characters fall in love out of a feeling of detachment from others, crystallize an imaginative ideal of their beloved, and organize their entire life around this object of desire.

[24] Henry James, unsigned review of William Morris' *"The Earthly Paradise,"* 358-361.

[25] As Rougemont observes, courtly lovers die in order to achieve a total spiritual union, which is impossible on earth; they ascend to an "ultimate union with light, something far beyond any love attainable in this life," p. 76.

[26] Mario Praz, *The Romantic Agony*, p. 247.

[27] Quoted by Edel, *The Untried Years*, p. 164.

[28] Edel argues that James sensed a latent vampirism in his relationship with Minny Temple and that he embodied this idea in "Poor Richard" and "Longstaff's Marriage." The interpretation hinges upon a passage in a letter James wrote to William shortly after Minny's death: "Among the sad reflections that her death provokes for me, there is none sadder than this view of the gradual change and reversal in our relations: I slowly crawling from weakness and inaction and suffering into strength and health and hope: she sinking out of brightness and youth into decline and death [Edel, *The Untried Years*, p. 326]." Edel interprets these lines too literally, perhaps. It is doubtful that, at this point in his career, James believed one person could draw life from another (though he sees it as a general, if not a literal, truth years later in *The Sacred Fount*). Psychological vampirism implies a fusion of two minds, which is incompatible with James' early belief in man's subjective isolation.

[29] James, "Our Mutual Friend," p. 787.

[30] Edel, *The Untried Years*, p. 211.

[31] Leon Edel, *Henry James: The Conquest of London*, p. 177.

[32] James, *Roderick Hudson*, p. 66. All subsequent passages will be cited in text.

[33] Quoted in Edel, *The Conquest of London*, p. 168.

[34] James, *Letters*, 1:72.

[35] Henry James, *Hawthorne*, pp. 47-48.

[36] Henry James, "Honore de Balzac," *Galaxy* 20 (December 1875):827.

[37] James, *Letters*, 1:69.

[38] Edel, *The Conquest of London*, p. 338.

[39] Ibid., p. 339.

[40] Erik Erikson, *Identity: Youth and Crisis*, p. 23.

[41] Ibid.

THREE: Requirements of the Imagination

[1] James, *The Art of the Novel*, p. 42.

[2] Henry James, *The Portrait of a Lady*, 2 vols., in *The Novels and Tales of Henry James*, vols. 3 and 4, 1:69. All further references will be cited in text by volume and page. Volume numbers for all two-volume novels will be listed as 1 or 2.

[3] James, *The Art of the Novel*, pp. 51-53.

[4] Erikson, p. 50.

[5] Dorothea Krook, *The Ordeal of Consciousness in Henry James*, p. 50.

[6] Henry James, *The Bostonians*, p. 293.

[7] Henry James, *The Reverberator*, in *Americans and Europe*, p. 256.

[8] Henry James, *The Princess Casamassima*, 2 vols., in *Novels and Tales*, vols. 5 and 6, 2:263. All further references will be cited in text by volume and page.

[9] James, *The Art of the Novel*, p. 60.

[10] Lionel Trilling points out that James did not envision an orderly Marxian revolution:

> There is no upsurge of an angry proletariat led by a disciplined party which plans to head a new strong state. Such a revolution has its conservative aspect—it seeks to save certain elements of bourgeois culture for its own use, for example, science and the means of production and even some social agencies. The revolutionary theory of *The Princess Casamassima* has little in common with this. There is no organized mass movement; there is no disciplined party but only a strong conspiratorial center. There are no plans for taking over the state and almost no ideas about the society of the future (pp. 68-69).

[11] James, *The Art of the Novel*, p. 60.

[12] Trilling, p. 86.

[13] M. E. Grenander, in tracing the development of Christina Light, observes that she has become disillusioned, cynical, and petulant by the time we see her in *The Princess Casamassima*. "Henry James's *Capricciosa*, Christina Light in *Roderick Hudson* and *The Princess Casamassima*," pp. 309-319.

[14] Trilling, pp. 68-74.

[15] James, *Letters*, 1:124.

FOUR: The Disturbed Midnight

[1] Leon Edel, *Henry James: The Treacherous Years*, p. 350.

[2] James, *Letters*, 1:356.

[3] Edel, *The Treacherous Years*, p. 83.

[4] Ibid.

[5] Desmond MacCarthy, *Portraits*, p. 151.

[6] Edel, *The Treacherous Years*, p. 140.

[7] James, *Letters*, 1:101.

[8] Edel, *The Treacherous Years*, p. 350.

[9] Pater, p. 157.

[10] Edel, *The Treacherous Years*, pp. 175-176.

[11] MacCarthy, p. 154.

[12] Henry James, *In the Cage and Other Tales*, p. 176. See text for all further references.

[13] William James, *Pragmatism*, p. 36.

[14] James, *Letters*, 2:83.

[15] William James, *Pragmatism*, p. 37.

[16] James, *The Art of the Novel*, p. 5.

[17] James, *Letters*, 1:222.

[18] For a more detailed commentary on James' relation to aestheticism, see Chapter Two of this study, also Viola Hopkins Winner's brief but illuminating remarks in *Henry James and the Visual Arts*, pp. 45-47.

[19] James, *Letters*, 1:222.

[20] Although *The Sense of the Past* was not published until 1917, James began working on the novel during the winter of 1899-1900.

[21] Pater, p. 157.

[22] James, *Letters*, 1:334.

[23] Henry James, *The Awkward Age*, in *Novels and Tales*, 9:8. See text for further references.

[24] In his provocative reading of the novel, Strother Purdy compares Longdon to Nabokov's Humbert Humbert. See *The Hole in the Fabric: Science, Contemporary Literature, and Henry James*, pp. 139-148. Although both James' and Nabokov's heroes are "solipsistic artist creators," Purdy's contention that Longdon "burns with the same [erotic] fires that consume Humbert Humbert," and takes Nanda to his estate at the end of the novel to celebrate a "sexual mystery" is highly improbable. Longdon speaks of both himself and Nanda as dead, and he is so horrified at the libertinism of Mrs. Brook's circle that he goes back into hibernation. Although there may be a muted eroticism in the image worship of some of James' other characters, none of them ever consciously seek sexual union with their love object. This fact serves to distinguish them from such other romantic idealists as Julien Sorel, Emma Bovary, Charles Swann, Hans Castorp, and Humbert Humbert, among others.

[25] T. S. Eliot, "Portrait of a Lady," *Collected Poems: 1909-1962*, p. 12.

[26] James, *Letters*, 1:333.

[27] Edel, *The Treacherous Years*, p. 258.

[28] T. S. Eliot, *The Cocktail Party*, p. 138.

[29] Robert Browning, "Evelyn Hope" (1855) l. 128.

[30] Henry James, *The Sense of the Past*, p. 48. See text for all further references.

[31] James, *Letters*, 1:351.

[32] Ibid., p. 359.

[33] James, *Notebooks*, p. 299.

[34] Ibid., p. 300.

[35] Ibid., p. 362.

[36] Ibid., p. 364.

[37] Ibid., p. 365.

[38] There is some dispute as to exactly where James discontinued his original draft of *The Sense of the Past* in early 1900. Lubbock and Matthiessen agree that he stopped "in the middle of the scene between Ralph and the Ambassador," or after "two and a half sections." Leon Edel, however, claims in his biography that James had completed three full sections or chapters before he set the manuscript aside during the first months of 1900. I base my concurrence with Lubbock and Matthiessen upon James' own remark, in his 1914 notes, that he stopped at a point where a "bridge" between past and present was needed. By the end of chapter three, this bridge is already established—the alter ego has mysteriously descended from the portrait and set off to explore modern London, while Ralph stands on his own doorstep with an awareness that he is about to walk into the world of 1820. It seems doubtful that James would have brought his protagonist to the brink of his adventures, with only a door standing between him and the past, and then dropped him. It seems more probable, both from a technical and a psychological point of view, that a struggling James abandoned his manuscript in the middle of Ralph's attempt to describe who he actually is.

[39] James, *Notebooks*, pp. 298-299.

[40] Percy Lubbock, Preface to Henry James' *The Sense of the Past*.

[41] Henry James, *The Sacred Fount*, p. 191. See text for further references.

[42] Edel, *The Treacherous Years*, p. 339.

[43] West, p. 108.

[44] Krook, p. 167.

[45] James, *Notebooks*, pp. 150-151.

[46] Leon Edel, *Henry James: The Master*, p. 70.

FIVE: A Practical Fusion

[1] Although James does not allude to either incident directly, he grew up under the influence of his father's mystical religion and had several discussions with William about psychic phenomenon. Since the work of both Henry Sr. and William

arose out of their own terrifying experiences, it seems highly probable that Henry, in his intimate relation, would have learned about them. His own lifelong interest in ghost stories, from "The Romance of Certain Old Clothes" (1868) to "The Jolly Corner" (1908), supports this supposition. Henry also had direct knowledge of the mysterious psychological disturbances of his sister, Alice, who exhibited suicidal tendencies during her periodic nervous breakdowns. William wrote to her in 1891 that she was victimized by the conflicting "split-up selves," which psychical research was bringing to light. Henry was also aware that his sister was dominated by two very different personalities at different times. Like William, he loved and pitied her; realizing that something prevented her from fully cultivating the best part of herself, he held that, but for her neurotic lapses, she might have become one of the most remarkable women in Europe. See Trilling, p. 79n.

[2] Quoted by Edel in *The Untried Years*, p. 30.

[3] William James, *Varieties of Religious Experience*, p. 138.

[4] William James, *Varieties of Religious Experience*, pp. 375-376.

[5] Ibid., p. 146.

[6] Ibid., p. 376.

[7] James, *Notebooks*, p. 182.

[8] Ibid.

[9] Henry James, "The Beast in the Jungle," in *Complete Tales*, 10:401.

[10] Banta, p. 155.

[11] William James, "What Psychical Research Has Accomplished," in *William James on Psychical Research*, p. 27.

[12] William James, *Proceedings of the Society for Psychical Research*, in *William James on Psychical Research*, pp. 112-113.

[13] William James, *Psychical Research*, p. 101.

[14] James, *Notes on Novelists*, p. 237.

[15] Henry James, *The Golden Bowl*, in *Novels and Tales*, 23:371.

[16] Henry James, *Confidence*, p. 196.

[17] James, *Roderick Hudson*, p. 253.

[18] Henry James, *The Tragic Muse*, in *Novels and Tales*, 8:69.

[19] Henry James, *What Maisie Knew*, in *Novels and Tales*, 11:9.

[20] Henry James, *The Ambassadors*, in *Novels and Tales*, 21:133.

[21] James, *The Portrait of a Lady*, in *Novels and Tales*, 4:418.

[22] Lebowitz, p. 66.

[23] Appignanesi, p. 22.

[24] James, *The Ambassadors*, in *Novels and Tales*, 22:83.

[25] Ibid., 21:65.

[26] Ibid., 218.

[27] Ibid., 22:6-7.

[28] See J. A. Ward, "*The Ambassadors* as Conversion Experience."

[29] James, *The Ambassadors*, in *Novels and Tales*, 22:276.

[30] Henry James, *The Wings of the Dove*, 2 vols., in *Novels and Tales*, vols. 19 and 20, 1:48. Further references are cited by volume and page number in text.

[31] See Lebowitz, pp. 62-66.

[32] James, *The Art of the Novel*, p. 299.

[33] William James, *Varieties of Religious Experience*, p. 152.

[34] Sigmund Freud, *The Basic Writings of Sigmund Freud*, p. 618.

[35] Thomas Mann, "Tonio Kröger," in *Death in Venice and Seven Other Stories*, p. 85.

[36] Quoted from John Unterecker, *A Readers' Guide to W. B. Yeats* (New York: Noonday, 1959), p. 27.

[37] Ibid., p. 12.

[38] D. H. Lawrence, "New Heaven and Earth," in *The Complete Poems of D. H. Lawrence*, p. 256.

[39] Ibid.

[40] D. H. Lawrence, *Women in Love*, pp. 8-9.

[41] Ibid., pp. 84-85.

[42] See Cecil Y. Lang, "Romantic Chemistry."

[43] Rougemont, p. 76.

[44] D. H. Lawrence, *Studies in Classic American Literature*, p. 182.

[45] James, "Gabriele D'Annunzio," *Notes on Novelists*, pp. 289-290.

[46] Ibid., pp. 292-293.

[47] Henry James, "Is there a Life after Death?" p. 201.

[48] Ibid., p. 233.

[49] Henry James, *Henry James' Letters*, p. 226.

[50] Quoted by F. O. Matthiessen in *Henry James: The Major Phase*, p. 47.

[51] James, *Autobiography*, p. 544.

[52] Lawrence, *Women in Love*, p. 193.

[53] D. H. Lawrence, "A Propos of *Lady Chatterley's Lover*," p. 100.

[54] James, *The Art of the Novel*, p. 46.

[55] D. H. Lawrence, "Morality and the Novel," p. 530.

SIX: For Love

[1] Appignanesi, p. 27.

[2] C. G. Jung, "The Phenomenology of the Spirit in Fairy Tales," in *The Archetypes of the Collective Unconscious, Collected Works*, pp. 207-254.

[3] James, *The Golden Bowl*, 2 vols., in *Novels and Tales*, vols. 23 and 24, 2:4. All further quotations will be cited by volume and page in the text.

[4] The Brothers Grimm, *Grimm's Fairy Tales* (New York and London: Harper and Brothers, 1912), p. 61.

[5] James, *Notebooks*, p. 131.

[6] Ibid.

NOTES, CHAPTER SIX

[7] Edel, *The Master*, pp. 210-211.

[8] Freud, p. 618.

[9] R. P. Blackmur, Introduction to Henry James' *The Golden Bowl*, p. 8.

[10] Henry James' "A Round of Visits," *The Complete Tales*, 12:434. All further quotations from James' tales in this chapter are taken from *Complete Tales*, vol. 12, and will be cited by page number.

[11] Henry James, *The American Scene*, pp. 72-95.

[12] Ibid., pp. 75-76. For a fuller and more illuminating study of James' sense of cultural alienation at this time, see F. O. Matthiessen, pp. 107-111.

[13] James, *The American Scene*, p. 91.

[14] James, *Letters*, 2:360-361.

Anderson, Quentin. *The American Henry James*. New Brunswick: Rutgers University Press, 1957.

Appignanesi, Lisa. *Femininity and the Creative Imagination*. London: Vision Press, 1973.

Auden, W. H. "The American Scene." *The Dyer's Hand and Other Essays*. New York: Vintage, 1948.

Banta, Martha. *Henry James and the Occult*. Bloomington: Indiana University Press, 1972.

Beerbohm, Max. "Jacobean and Shavian." *Around Theatres*. London: Rupert Hart-Davis, 1930.

Bettelheim, Bruno. *The Uses of Enchantment: The Meaning and Significance of Fairy Tales*. New York: Knopf, 1976.

Blackmur, Richard P. Introduction to *The Golden Bowl*, by Henry James. New York: Dell, 1963.

Brooks, Van Wyck. *The Pilgrimage of Henry James*. New York: E. P. Dutton & Company, 1925.

Cargill, Oscar. *The Novels of Henry James*. New York: Macmillan, 1961.

Dupee, F. W., ed. *The Question of Henry James*. New York: Holt, 1948.

Edel, Leon. *Henry James: The Conquest of London*. Philadelphia: Lippincott, 1962.

———. *Henry James: The Master*. Philadelphia: Lippincott, 1972.

———. *Henry James: The Middle Years*. Philadelphia: Lippincott, 1962.

———. *Henry James: The Treacherous Years*. Philadelphia: Lippincott, 1969.

———. *Henry James: The Untried Years*. London: Rupert Hart-Davis, 1953.

———. Introduction to *The Sacred Fount*, by Henry James. London: Rupert Hart-Davis, 1959.

Eliot, T. S. *The Cocktail Party*. New York: Harcourt, Brace & World, 1950.

———. *Collected Poems: 1909-1962*. New York: Harcourt, Brace & World, 1962.

Erikson, Erik. *Identity: Youth and Crisis*. New York: Norton, 1968.

BIBLIOGRAPHY

Fiedler, Leslie. *Love and Death in the American Novel*. New York: Criterion Books, 1960.

Freud, Sigmund. *The Basic Writings of Sigmund Freud*. Edited by A. A. Brill. New York: Modern Library, 1938.

Gard, Roger, ed. *Henry James: The Critical Heritage*. London: Routledge and Kegan Paul, 1968.

Geismar, Maxwell. *Henry James and the Jacobites*. Boston: Houghton Mifflin, 1963.

Graham, Kenneth. *Henry James: The Drama of Fulfillment*. Oxford: Clarendon Press, 1975.

Green, Graham. "Henry James: The Private Universe." In *The English Novelists*, edited by Derek Verschoyle, pp. 215-228. London: Chatto & Windus, 1936.

Grenander, M. E. "Henry James's *Capricciosa*: Christina Light in *Roderick Hudson* and *The Princess Casamassima*." *PMLA* 75 (June 1960):309-319.

Hatch, Eric. "Henry James and The Aesthetic Movement." Ph.D. dissertation, University of Virginia, 1974.

Henley, W. E. "Review." *Academy* 14 (October 1878):354-355.

Hough, Graham. *The Last Romantics*. New York: Barnes and Noble, 1947.

James, Alice. *The Diary of Alice James*. New York: Dodd and Mead, 1964.

James, Henry. *The American Scene*. London: Chapman and Hall, 1907.

————. *Americans and Europe*. Edited by Napier Wilt and John Lucas. Boston: Houghton Mifflin, 1965.

————. *The Art of the Novel: Critical Prefaces by Henry James*. Edited by Richard P. Blackmur. New York: Scribner's, 1934.

————. *Autobiography*. Edited by Frederick W. Dupee. New York: Criterion Books, 1956.

————. *The Bostonians*. Harmondsworth: Penguin, 1966.

————. *The Complete Tales of Henry James*. Edited by Leon Edel. 12 vols. Philadelphia: Lippincott, 1964.

————. *Confidence*. New York: Universal Library, 1962.

————. "The Earthly Paradise." *The North American Review* 107 (July 1868):358-361.

————. *The Future of the Novel*. Edited by Leon Edel. New York: Vintage, 1956.

————. *Hawthorne*. New York: Collier, 1966.

BIBLIOGRAPHY

————. *Henry James' Letters*. Edited by Leon Edel. Vol. 1. Cambridge: Cambridge University Press, 1974.

————. *In the Cage and Other Tales*. Edited by Morton Dauwen Zabel. New York: Norton, 1958.

————. "Is there a Life after Death?" *After Days: Thoughts on the Future Life*. New York and London: Harper & Brothers, 1910.

————. *The Letters of Henry James*. Edited by Percy Lubbock. 2 vols. New York: Scribner's, 1920.

————. *Literary Reviews and Essays*. Edited by Albert Mordell. New York: Twayne, 1957.

————. *The Novels and Tales of Henry James*. 24 vols. New York: Scribner's, 1907-1909.

————. *The Notebooks of Henry James*. Edited by F. O. Matthiessen and Kenneth B. Murdock. New York: Oxford University Press, 1947.

————. *Notes and Reviews*. Cambridge: Dunster House, 1921.

————. *Notes on Novelists*. New York: Scribner's, 1914.

————. "Our Mutual Friend." *The Nation* 1 (21 December 1865):787-789.

————. *The Painter's Eye*. Edited by John L. Sweeney. Cambridge: Harvard University Press, 1956.

————. *Roderick Hudson*. Boston: Houghton-Mifflin, 1875.

————. *The Sacred Fount*. London: Rupert Hart-Davis, 1959.

————. *The Sense of the Past*. Edited by Percy Lubbock. New York: Scribner's, 1917.

James, William. *Pragmatism and Other Essays*. New York: Washington Square, 1963.

————. *Principles of Psychology*. 2 vols. New York: Henry Holt Company, 1890.

————. *The Varieties of Religious Experience*. New York: Collier, 1961.

————. *William James on Psychical Research*. Edited by Gardner Murphy and Robert O. Ballou. New York: Viking, 1960.

Jung, C. G. *The Archetypes of the Collective Unconscious*. Vol. 9 of *Collected Works*. Bollingen Series, no. 20. Princeton: Princeton University Press, 1963.

Kelley, Cornelia Pulsifer. *The Early Development of Henry James*. Urbana: University of Illinois Press, 1930.

Kraft, James. *The Early Tales of Henry James*. Carbondale: Southern Illinois Press, 1969.

BIBLIOGRAPHY

Krook, Dorothea. *The Ordeal of Consciousness in Henry James*. Cambridge: Cambridge University Press, 1962.

Lang, Cecil Y. "Romantic Chemistry." *The Courier* 10 (April 1973):35-46.

Langbaum, Robert. *The Modern Spirit: Essays on the Continuity of Nineteenth and Twentieth Century Literature*. New York: Oxford University Press, 1970.

Lawrence, D. H. "A Propos of *Lady Chatterley's Lover*." *Sex, Literature and Censorship*. New York: Viking, 1959.

———. *The Complete Poems of D. H. Lawrence*. Edited by Vivian de Sola Pinto. New York: Viking, 1973.

———. "Morality and the Novel." *Phoenix*. New York: Viking, 1936.

———. *Studies in Classic American Literature*. New York: Penguin, 1976.

———. *Women in Love*. New York: Viking, 1972.

Lebowitz, Naomi. *The Imagination of Loving*. Detroit: Wayne State University Press, 1965.

Lubbock, Percy. *The Craft of Fiction*. New York: Viking, 1921.

MacCarthy, Desmond. *Portraits*. London: Macmillan, 1949.

MacKenzie, Manfred. *Communities of Honor and Love in Henry James*. Cambridge: Harvard University Press, 1976.

Mann, Thomas. *Death in Venice and Seven Other Stories*. New York: Vintage, 1963.

Matthiessen, F. O. *Henry James: The Major Phase*. New York: Oxford University Press, 1944.

Miller, J. Hillis. *Thomas Hardy: Distance and Desire*. Cambridge: Harvard University Press, 1970.

Nowell-Smith, Simon. *The Legend of the Master*. New York: Scribner's, 1948.

Ortega y Gasset, Jose. *On Love: Aspects of a Single Theme*. Translated by Toby Talbot. New York: New American Library, 1957.

Pater, Walter. *The Renaissance*. New York: New American Library, 1959.

Praz, Mario. *The Romantic Agony*. London: Oxford University Press, 1933.

Purdy, Strother. *The Hole in the Fabric: Science, Contemporary Literature, and Henry James*. Pittsburgh: University of Pittsburgh Press, 1977.

BIBLIOGRAPHY

Rougemont, Denis de. *Love in the Western World*. New York: Harper and Row, 1956. First published as *L'amour et l'occident*, 1940.

Stendhal. *Love*. Translated by Gilbert and Suzanne Sale. Harmondsworth: Penguin. 1975.

Thurber, James. "The Wings of Henry James." *Lanterns and Lances*. New York: Harper, 1961, pp. 90-111.

Trilling, Lionel. *The Liberal Imagination*. New York: Viking, 1950.

Ward, J. A. "*The Ambassadors* as Conversion Experience," *The Southern Review*, no. 2 (Spring 1969):350-374.

Wells, H. G. *Boon, The Mind of the Race, The Wild Asses of the Devil, and The Last Trump*. New York: G. H. Doran, 1915.

West, Rebecca. *Henry James*. New York: Henry Holt & Company, 1916.

Wharton, Edith. *A Backward Glance*. New York: Scribner's, 1964.

Wilson, Edmund, "The Pilgrimage of Henry James." *The Shores of Light*. New York: Farrar, Straus & Young, 1952, pp. 217-228.

Winner, Viola Hopkins. *Henry James and the Visual Arts*. Charlottesville: University of Virginia Press, 1970.

Yeats, W. B. *The Collected Poems*. New York: Macmillan, 1956.

Library of Congress Cataloging in Publication Data

Sicker, Philip.
Love and the quest for identity in the fiction
of Henry James.

Bibliography: p.
Includes index
1. James, Henry, 1843-1916—Criticism and interpretation.
2. Love in literature.
3. Identity (Psychology) in literature.   I. Title.
PS2127.L65S5   813'.4   79-17311
ISBN 0-691-06417-2
ISBN 0-691-01366-7 pbk.